Sex, Lies and Stereotypes

Challenging Views of Women, Men and Relationships

Dr Gary W. Wood

NH
NEW HOLLAND

Dedicated to 28 February 2000 and 'A Case of You'

First published in 2005 by New Holland Publishers (UK) Ltd
London · Cape Town · Sydney · Auckland

www.newhollandpublishers.com

Garfield House, 86–88 Edgware Road, London W2 2EA, United Kingdom

80 McKenzie Street, Cape Town 8001, South Africa

14 Aquatic Drive, Frenchs Forest, NSW 2086, Australia

218 Lake Road, Northcote, Auckland, New Zealand

ISBN 1 84330 894 0

Publishing Manager: Jo Hemmings
Senior Editor: Kate Michell
Editor: Deborah Taylor
Assistant Editor: Rose Hudson
Cover Design: Ian Hughes
Icon Design: Ian Hughes & Dr Gary W. Wood
Design: Nicky Barneby
Production: Joan Woodroffe

Reproduction by Modern Age Repro House Ltd, Hong Kong
Printed and bound by Replika Press PVT Ltd, India

Acknowledgements

I wish to acknowledge my gratitude to all who helped directly or indirectly with this book, including everyone who asked 'How's the book coming along?'. More specifically I would like to acknowledge:

Jo Hemmings, Kate Michell, Yvonne Thynne and everyone at New Holland for their hard work.

Vicky Lyne who read over the first draft, made corrections and helpful suggestions.

Jan 'Demon' Deeming for her support during this project.

My close friend and colleague Dr Petra Boynton for her ceaseless support, inspiration and encouragement.

Sue Rosten for doing my scanning and generally brightening my day.

Dr Neil Gittoes at University of Birmingham for answering my questions about hormones.

As some of this book is a development from my PhD. work, I'd like to thank Dr Roy Davies, Dr Dennis Howitt, Professor Rob Stammers, Dr Steve Westerman and data coder supreme Graham Miller.

Kate Bornstein, Martine Rothblatt and Riane Eisler whose work has been an inspiration to me.

Special thanks to Terry Chiu (Chong-Ping).

I'm not sure what they would have made of it, but I dedicate this book to the memory of my grandparents: Nellie Florence Butcher (née Balnaves), Clifford Bertram Butcher, Lilie Wood (née Trueman) and William George Wood, and to each and every member of my family.

Contents

PART THREE:
Changing Views: Colour Vision

Introduction

The Doors of Perception

If the doors of perception were to be cleansed everything would appear to [humankind] as it is, infinite.
— William Blake, Romantic poet (1757–1827)

In order to change a colour it is enough to change the colour of its background — Michel Eugene Chevreul, chemist, philosopher and physicist (1786–1889)

WHO ARE YOU?

Dearly beloved, ladies and gentleman, I'd like you to consider:
Are you a real woman, a real man or something completely different?
Are you a new man or a new woman or a more traditional type?
Are you a lad, a geezer bird or a new lad or ladette?
Are you a husband, a wife, a partner or a lover?
Other half, better half, 'er indoors or significant other?
Are you a girlfriend, a boyfriend or just good friends?
Housewife, househusband, homemaker or home-wrecker?
Heartbroken or heartbreaker?
Giver, taker, earth-mover or faker?
Good lay, easy lay, goodtime girl or man about town?
Supervixen or medallion man?
Dating, mating or just anticipating?
Another Mrs Robinson or a sugar daddy?
Supermodel or superhero? Toy boy or trophy wife?
Are you an item, spoken for, on the market or just single?
Are you Arthur or Martha or Adam or Eve?
Batman or Robin or Thelma or Louise?

Are you masculine, feminine, undifferentiated or androgynous?
Polymorphously perverse or simply monogamous?
Are you a drag king, drag queen, transvestite or cross-dresser?
Hermaphrodite or intersexed, pre-op or post-op transsexual or
 transgendered?
Are you straight or gay, post-gay, straight-acting or gay for pay?
Are you a swinger or a one-night flinger? Bi-curious? Rent or trade?
Gay woman, lesbian or dyke? Butch or femme?
Are you 'one of us' or 'one of them'?
R U AC/DC or MSM? Or just a man who has sex with men?
Are you a virgin, or celibate or just ain't getting any?
Are you of minority status or just one of the many?
Are you a top or a bottom, are you active or passive?
Sadist or masochist? Dominant or submissive?
Are you a himbo, a bimbo, knees together or legs akimbo?
Heterosexual or homosexual? Pansexual or pomosexual?
Asexual, bisexual, omnisexual or *faux*mosexual?
Gender perfect, gender novice, gender outlaw or gender freak?
Are you one of the girls, one of the boys, one in a million or just one of
 the guys?
Or are you reading this somewhat at a loss,
Wondering who threw a firecracker in the dressing-up box?

Identity crisis

How, who and what are you? Why so many choices? When did it all get so complicated? What happened to 'pink for a girl' and 'blue for a boy' and the predictable sequence of roles and relationships that followed? This is not an unreasonable question, since research has demonstrated that many people find it difficult to interact with a baby unless they spot the tell-tale colour coding. Indeed, the labelling at birth of 'girl' or 'boy' – our *gender identity* – sets up a lifelong chain of expectations in terms of our behaviour, how we relate to others, our sexual encounters, prospective partners, economic prosperity and even our personality. This process, with all its ramifications, starts from birth. Experiments have shown that if a baby is dressed in pink, people are more likely to interact with it verbally, using expressions that emphasize the 'pretty little girl' before their eyes. However, if the same baby is dressed in blue, interactions are likely to be more physical in nature, with people emphasizing the 'big strong boy'. Same baby: different expectations.

We are often led to believe that men and women are so different that they may as well be from different planets. These differences are supposed to be hard-wired into our brains. Of course, it's easy to collect a few anecdotes and titbits of information to support this view. Different expectations produce different experiences and we see what we want to see.

Yet we would not expect to apply for a job where a ticked box (M or F) was all that employers needed to know about us, would we? Because how, with just one stroke of the pen, could we possibly convey our personality, skills, ambitions, our suitability for the job and the likelihood of succeeding in specific tasks? Maybe, to err on the side of caution, we could tick a couple of boxes to indicate our race, age and perhaps sexuality, too. The whole process need only take about five minutes, and make job application as well as candidate selection far easier and cheaper. We wouldn't waste time trying for jobs we weren't 'born' to do.

Far from being an attractive prospect, this sounds like a nightmarish vision of the future from a science-fiction movie. After all, aren't there supposed to be laws to protect us from that kind of thing? Aren't we meant to be trying to bring an end to discrimination?

So, how is it that we can comfortably hold these two seemingly conflicting views of male and female roles: different planets on one hand and equal rights on the other? With this in mind, let me rephrase the question: *In what ways are you one of the girls, one of the boys, one in a million or just one of the guys?*

Romantic spin

I checked the weather forecast before going to bed. It was encouraging so I decided to spend the whole of the next day working in the garden. I needed to weave all the ideas and questions spinning around in my head into an introduction for this book. After all, what better place could there be to ponder Adams and Eves, new and old, than my own little corner of Eden? Fancifully, I speculated that I would get up to watch the sunrise. Suitably inspired, I'd set the scene and map out the course of the book. As the day rolled by, I imagined watching the Sun course across the sky before seeing it sink beyond the horizon. What better inspiration could there be? After all, there is something quite magical about sunrises and sunsets. Except that the Sun never really sets, the Sun doesn't rise or move across the sky or set. The Earth turns! Everything else is just a perceptual illusion.

Sex, Lies and Stereotypes

So what's the connection between relationships and sunrises, sunsets or any other aspect of astronomy? Well, we make this connection every time we claim that men and women are so different that they may as well be from different planets. This metaphor seems so ingrained in our collective psyche that it is worth further exploration. At a certain point, our ancestors faced a crossroads. Research had amassed and demanded a revision of the prevailing view that the Earth was flat and the Sun went round it. This view was no longer sustainable and a scientific revolution followed. We are at a similar crossroads today with our attitudes to the roles and identities of women and men. Like it or not, we too are on the brink of a revolution and the 'different planet' approach is a diversion from our progress in the fields of human rights, equal opportunities and civil liberties.

Sunsets and sunrises imply that the Sun moves round the Earth, but the fact is that the Earth moves round the Sun. We've known this for a few hundred years. However, a few forward-thinking people were once almost burned at the stake for even suggesting it. The idea of sunrises and sunsets belongs to a view of the world that comes from the past, but is a far too romantic notion to let go. What we are really talking about is how it is possible to have different perceptions of the same thing, even something as fundamental as the nature of the universe. There is a strong parallel between our understanding of sunrises and sunsets and how we view the roles of women, men and relationships. It's a case of 'head' versus 'heart'. We know the science but crave the comfort of the romantic 'spin'.

Colour vision

During the 20th century, social changes brought about a marked convergence in the roles and rights of men and women in Western societies. Yet, here we are in the 21st century still talking about women and men as if they come from alien worlds. Pushing aside the obvious entertainment value of this, if we look at the facts there is no other creature on the planet as similar to women as men. We know this as scientific fact, yet we find comfort in the romantic fiction.

The Earth-centred universe and the 'different planets' view of relationships are, of course, simplifications. They are based on the limited but predictable worldview we get from our comfort zone. Although we may talk about just sitting back and watching the world go by, sometimes it just passes us by. Maybe you found the opening poem a little bewildering. It may contrast sharply with your own experiences; some of the roles, identities and relationships may be familiar to you, while others may be quite alien. Nevertheless, they do exist. Some people may define themselves and live their lives in ways that we hadn't even considered, and yet we may have more in common with them than with our next-door neighbour.

The M or F on your birth certificate is not a guarantee of a shared vision. Has the world become more complicated or is there more opportunity for expression? Are you constrained or liberated? Would it be simpler if we all went back to the values of the 1950s? After all, those old black-and-white films are so much more romantic. Aren't they?

We are living in flux. For some people this provokes a powerful knee-jerk reaction, a hankering for the certainty that is often represented by tradition: a golden age, the halcyon days. Do we really want to return to an age where everyone knew their place, even though many people had little choice on the matter? We certainly had predictability then. However, no matter how much things seem to have changed, they didn't change overnight. It's not as if yesterday the world was in black and white, and we woke up one day to find we'd all become Technicolor. Things constantly change and evolve and they are never as fixed as they seem – nor as fixed as we would like. Change seems to creep up on as when we aren't looking. So, often we see what we expect to see, until something shakes our perceptions. We live in a perpetual state of potentiality, always becoming. Sometimes we just get so caught up in the routine so we don't see it.

The film *Pleasantville* (1998) beautifully documented the sexual and political awakening of a fictional town in 1950s America, from black-and-white certainty, to the celebration of Technicolor variety and diversity. In the real world, such progress has only been made by individuals, groups and whole societies who dared to step outside their comfort zone, preferring to fight for change rather than what they were used to. Standing on the shoulders of these pioneers, we continue to aspire to an ideal of equal opportunities, even if these aspirations sometimes shake the very foundations of our lives. In truth, they are just growing pains.

I 'filter', therefore I am

Popular psychology often states that it is our perception that creates our reality. This notion is founded on academic psychology, which reveals that human perception is not a passive process. More information than we can possibly process comes at us from every direction every moment of the day. If we tried to process every tiny bit of information it would cause total mental overload. Instead, we make sense of it all by using a kind of filter that only lets through anything that is important to us, which means we are active rather than passive processors.

The filters through which we view the world are based on a variety of personal factors: expectations within our culture, upbringing, individual tastes, motivations, life experiences and even moods. These factors combine to form our personal perceptual filters. Thus we each perceive the world in a slightly different way. Think about our taste in clothes, décor, our sense of humour and so on. Think about how one person may see a situation as a problem whereas someone else may view it as an opportunity. We even talk about people who view the world through rose-tinted spectacles, indicating that they have an overly optimistic view of the world that comes from seeing only the good and filtering out the bad. We recognize it every time someone talks about the past as if it were a golden age.

In the 'honeymoon' phase of a relationship, we view everything through a 'similarity filter'. We actively seek out all the things that we have in common with the other person. At the same time, we filter out many of the differences. Much later on in the relationship, we start to focus on the differences instead. Sometimes we panic and accuse the other person of changing – and sometimes they have changed, but more often it's our filter that has changed. Not surprisingly, we get what we search for and the 'evidence' mounts to support our belief that we are 'drifting apart'. In reality, what we are experiencing is the process of balance. This emphasizes two crucial ways that we make sense of the world as human beings. Firstly, we are often drawn to all-or-nothing, either/or and black-and-white solutions, e.g. we are 'in love' or 'all out of love', we find it difficult to tolerate shades of grey. Secondly, we are 'pattern seekers': once we have a pet theory, we use this as a filter for our perceptions, so we begin to look for consistent patterns, even if it means overlooking (filtering out) evidence to the contrary.

Invariably, when faced with two extremes, the solution lies in the shades of grey, even though our reaction is to look for the black-and-white solution. For instance, we could pretend that our partner is from a different planet to us and live our lives like stereotypical characters from a 1950s soap opera. Of course it could work, if all the actors play along and follow the script. However, as Albert Einstein argued, it is unlikely that we will find the solution to our problems by using the same level of thinking that created them. Sometimes it helps to take a holiday from our view of the world.

Travel guide: Sex, lies and stereotypes

We are told that nothing broadens the mind like travel. This doesn't have to be physical travel and we certainly don't need to go into outer space. We just need to consider an alternative perception to gain a different experience of something. If you take visitors around your home town, it's curious how you can start getting excited about things you normally take for granted. Now, clearly these things didn't change overnight, it is your new perception of trying to see things through the eyes of someone else that changes your experience.

In *Sex, Lies and Stereotypes* old concepts and ideas surrounding the roles of women and men and the nature of human relationships will be revisited. Rather than a rulebook, consider this a travel guide. If you don't like it, then you can always go home afterwards to your personal comforts. Alternatively, you may decide you like a few aspects of what you've seen, and choose to take them back with you. That's fine, too. The choice is yours. Overall, the main aim of the book is to shed a new or different light on the changing views of women, men and relationships and to separate some of the scientific facts from the science fiction. We will still look at contributions from popular psychology and contrast them with 'down-to-earth' accounts of more cutting-edge research. Much of it will surprise you.

The book has three parts. The first – **Different Planets and Black Holes** – takes a critical look at the traditional view of women, men and relationships. It offers an alternative gender mythology, takes a closer look at the popular-psychology approach to gender and explores academic psychology. This section raises the stakes and moves away from the twilight world of fairytales by offering definitions of key terms in debates on sex and gender. It offers an explanation of why the 'different planet' approach to gender and relationships appeals to us and explores gender stereotypes in greater depth.

In the second section – **Back to Basics** – we do just that, go right back to our beginnings and review basic human biology and gender differences. We find that male and female differences are overstated to the cost of our similarities. It offers some guidelines for critically assessing research, books and media sources (including this one). We also look at the mental and physical health implications of living according to rigid gender roles.

In the third section – **Changing Views: Colour Vision** – we consider some alternative views of human relationships; offer advice for assessing and improving communication skills, and reframing relationships in a more co-operative light; and, finally, consider the impact of changing views of gender and relationships on other aspects of our lives, such as our attitudes to sex and sexuality.

Sex, Lies and Stereotypes ends with the conclusion: men are from Earth and women are from Earth, and it's high time we got over it. It is time to embrace our similarities and focus on building relationships based on partnership not 'alien-nation'.

Personal perceptual filters

The opening quotation by the poet William Blake suggests that that we all have limitations on our perceptions. The quotation from Michel Euguene Chevreul, although talking about art, can easily be applied to our view of life. Our social, cultural, political and economic backgrounds colour the way we view the world. Indeed, this introduction acts as a filter with which to read this book – it sets the scene and describes the limits of inquiry. The book, in turn, is offered as a compensatory filter to the way we view the roles of women, men and relationships.

Some of the concepts already outlined may have provoked some thoughts, feeling and emotions from you. As you read through the book you may experience a knee-jerk reaction to some of the material. Some of the ideas might be met with total disbelief. This is just your personal perceptual filter kicking in. It is not surprising, since at the heart of this book is the question 'Who are you?'. For now, I ask you simply to acknowledge the feeling and make a note of it. To gain the most from this book, simply 'suspend your disbelief' until the end. Whatever your final verdict, I hope you enjoy the journey.

PART ONE

Different Planets and Black Holes

1

The Great Divide: It's All Here in Black and White

The difference between fiction and reality? Fiction has to make sense – Tom Clancy, novelist (b.1947)

When you gaze long into the abyss, the abyss also gazes into you – Freiderich Nietzsche, philosopher (1844–1900)

PREVIEW

In this chapter we will:

* Consider an alternative mythology for the roles of women, men and human relationships.
* Examine definitions of key technical terms within the areas of sex, gender and sexuality.
* Discuss the 'black holes' in the 'different planet' approach to gender roles and human relationships.

Search and re-search

My research for this book involved a wide range of sources in order to gain the fullest picture of the way we view the roles of women and men and human relationships. This may conjure up images of dusty library archives in which the researcher unearths a long-forgotten text by chance. This is an image we may have from the movies and, yes, sometimes it happens in real life too, only not as often as one might wish. Much of the material was familiar to me. I'd spent over three years of my life sifting the psychological wheat from the mythical chaff when conducting the research for my doctorate. Occasionally, however, I found myself making the odd detour through a few unfamiliar 'cornfields'. Sometimes I happened upon a barely-trodden path of enlightenment, but most often I stumbled upon some crop circles of dubious origin. A great deal of what we call science, as the 17th-century mathematician and physicist Isaac Newton said, is about 'standing on the shoulders of giants'. That is to say, that science is built on the discoveries or ideas of those who've gone before us. Unfortunately, when considering gender, sex and relationships, much of the work of the earthly intellectual giants is overlooked in favour of the little men from outer space.

THE GREAT DIVIDE

I'd *like* to tell you about the time I stumbled across an ancient text entitled *Corpus Cavernosum*. It's a rather meaty, hard-going volume that tells of two tribes of people, each tribe oblivious to the existence of the other, who inhabited opposite sites of a canyon, referred to as the Great Divide. The book was supposedly written by one of the tribes from the side of the canyon known as Sineplia. They were a proud, upstanding warrior race. They were great hunters, explorers and agriculturists. Technologically advanced, the Sineplians erected amazing tall, freestanding, pointed architectural monuments across their land.

By contrast, on the other side of the Great Divide, the people of Anigavlia, were more timid and inward-looking creatures. They cared little for technology and pointed things, being more interested in artistic pursuits and relationships. Somewhat shallow and vain people, they would while away the hours chatting, giggling, gazing into mirrors and grooming each other. Whereas the Sineplians were good at science and hard sums, the Anigavlians preferred to do a bit of colouring-in. Unlike the Sineplians, they never ever went over the edges. It is not an exaggeration to say that the

Sineplians and the Anigavlians were so different that they may as well have been from different planets: saturn and Neptune, Pluto and Mercury or any other interplanetary combination – take your pick.

One day, during a routine inspection of their hi-tech surveillance towers, a uniformed Sineplian engineer noticed a rustling in the bushy undergrowth on the other side of the abyss. After a rational discussion with his fellow engineers, they decided to instigate a scientific observation of the land across the Great Divide. It was not long before their equipment had captured images of the Anigavlians going about their business, or rather their sheer lack of it.

The Anigavlians had always harboured a secret desire to be the objects of desire for such technologically advanced strangers. Nevertheless, they were a little annoyed that they hadn't been given more notice. They scurried off for a couple of years (or what seemed like it) and devised alluring apparel and cosmetic enhancements. They also trimmed the bushy undergrowth lining the Great Divide to afford the strangers a better view of their inane preening, tittering, frolicking and cavorting.

Soon, word got around that there was a bit of Anigavlian action on the other side. Lining the canyon, every full-blooded Sineplian stood proudly holding his impressive light-sabre in hand, vigorously waving their mighty weapons at the wondrous sight across the mighty chasm. The Anigavlians each had beautifully adorned baskets, and they ventured to the edge of the Great Divide, dipped their fingers into their baskets and threw spring flowers towards their admirers. Unfortunately, a few excitable trigger-happy Sineplians misinterpreted this as a hostile gesture and their light-sabres went off prematurely in their hands. Fortunately, none of the Anigavlians was seriously hurt.

Anyhow, the incident was soon forgotten on account of a bout of viral amnesia that was often known to sweep across their lands. Nevertheless, the coquettish floral display seemed to effect a chemical change in Sineplian blood and they all immediately fell in lust with the Anigavlians. Some of them seemed to lose all sense of rationality and they flung themselves headlong into the abyss. Their nether-regions seemed to take on minds of their own. Sineplian pride almost burst forth from their practical but rarely laundered undergarments.

However, unable to reach the objects of their desire, the Sineplians quickly pleasured themselves to temporarily cool their ardour. Once satisfied, they all fell asleep. This served to enrage the Anigavlians who up until this point had assumed that the fun was only just getting started. The next day when the Sineplians once again gathered on the edge of the crevice brandishing their weapons, the Anigavlians asked them to put them away and keep the noise down as they all had headaches. This in turn infuriated the Sineplians who immediately stormed off to their laboratories and invented a violent-looking harpoon thing. They shot big spiky things across the ravine and so began the invasion of Anigavlia.

At first the Anigavlians welcomed the Sineplian occupation and willingly shared the content of their baskets on a daily basis. Sineplians regaled them with wondrous tales of far-off lands and, although the Anigavlians suspected such tales to be as tall as Sineplian towers, they enjoyed them anyway. After a while, the Sineplians suggested that they should travel to these far-off lands. At first the Anigavlians resisted. However, always eager to put the feelings of others before themselves, they agreed to leave their ancestral homeland.

Across the Great Divide and onward they travelled and founded a new settlement. They decided to create a new name for a new beginning. From the word Sineplia, they took SINEP and from Anigavlia they took LIA, to create the new land of SINEPLIA. A few rebellious Anigavlians (the bookish ones) argued that the new name bore a startling similarity to the old Sineplia. Therefore, it was agreed to call the new settlement New Sineplia. This seemed to satisfy the rebellious Anigavlians who, for all of their bookishness, were still not 'the brightest buttons in the box'.

After a while both tribes seemed to forget about their very different and separate past lives, no doubt helped by yet further bouts of viral amnesia. They forgot that they were supposed to be different having come from opposite sides of the Great Divide. Therein lay the seeds of their future problems and frictions in their relationships. It also possibly had quite a lot to do with the Anigavlians in sensible shoes stirring up discontent too. Yes, of course, the bookish ones, who else?

Confession time

If you hadn't already guessed, this story is a thinly veiled parody of the 'different planet' approach to gender roles and relationships. This story is, as are many books that purport to be panaceas for relationships, purely fantasy – and the reality is far less sensational.

Ideas of gender roles were radically challenged during the 1960s and 1970s. By the 1980s most cutting-edge gender theorists were 'singing from the same hymn sheet'. By the early 1990s, there was a general consensus among the

Sex, Lies and Stereotypes

giants in the field that traditional gender-role stereotypes did more harm than good. Research during the 1980s and 1990s showed that adults viewed male and female gender-role stereotypes as overlapping categories.

But I suspect you still want to know more about the story of New Sineplia? We'll have a little more of the tale before we start to consider a few of the black holes in the narrative that even an epidemic of viral amnesia cannot obscure.

THE GREAT DISCONTENT

As soon as Sineplians and Anigavlians forgot that they were supposed to be different, cracks started to appear in their relationships. The Anigavlians began to get annoyed that the Sineplians were always working late in their laboratories and they protested that they too would like to get to grips with the wonders of modern technology. At first the Sineplians scoffed at the idea. However, after much persistence the Sineplians relented and invented a machine for washing undergarments. The Anigavlians were, mostly, delighted – the bookish ones had had their hearts set on a combine harvester. Nevertheless, they were happy to have some technology to play with. In one of the most romantic gestures ever recorded, the Sineplians feigned an attack of selective viral amnesia and pretended to forget how to operate the technology to wash their own undergarments. 'Look how much we need you. We'd be lost without you', the Sineplians said to their mates. This ruse worked for a while, but the fickleness of the Anigavlians, combined with having ideas above their station in life, meant that they soon tired of the machine for undergarment washing. They wanted more.

Panic spread among the Sineplians until a champion emerged from their ranks, a scholar of questionable credentials pieced together a manual for living together in harmony. It comprised a tale of two tribes, selective use of pseudo-science and a snappy title. It told of the time before New Sineplia and the bouts of viral amnesia, and how everything would be just fine if only Anigavlians would remember their place in the grand scheme of things and stuck to their respective scripts. The manual was distributed far and wide. And sure enough, like any quick-fix remedy, it worked for a while. But times had moved on and the respective roles between Sineplians and Anigavlians had changed. Ultimately, the manual was just papering over the cracks. It was time for a revolutionary rethink.

The End.

THE END?

That can't be the end! Surely we need a rewrite? But before we get too embroiled in the destiny of the Sineplians and the Anigavlians, maybe we should first consider our own destiny. Aren't we the victims of a premature ending in the story of female and male roles and relationships? Shouldn't we demand a rewrite for ourselves?

Of course that's not the final word on the Sineplians and Anigavlians and this book won't be the last word on men, women and relationships. Metaphors and allegories are useful devices for getting the point across – namely that men and women sometimes appear to be from different worlds. However, it's useless if their fictional quandary becomes intimately entwined and entangled with our own. At a certain point we have to separate the reality from the metaphor, and scientific fact from the science fiction. If we don't advance the thinking in some way we remain trapped in the abstract twilight world of fairytales.

In many ways there has never been so much information available about sex and relationships; unfortunately, much of it is based on stereotypes or designed purely for titillation. We are gripped simultaneously by fear and fascination. Researchers have described Western societies as 'sex-negative' cultures. That is to say that, even today, we consider sex to be a bit naughty, taboo, downright dirty, potentially dangerous and in need of regulation.

Literary scholar C.S. Lewis (1898–1963) observed that when we attempt to deal explicitly with sex, we must choose between the language of the nursery, the gutter or the anatomy class. If vocabulary is any indication of our desire to communicate about sex, then we seem desperate to do so. It has been estimated that we have over a thousand terms for the female and male genitals and the majority of them are indirect. Some sound as though they belong in the nursery, such as minky for a girl and winky for a boy. Some people choose to personalize their parts, by calling them Bessie, Mary, Fanny or Fiona, while men might choose from Peter, Percy, Willy or John Thomas. Animal metaphors are also popular with names such as beaver or pussy for a woman, and snake or weasel for a man. Monkey appears to be a unisex term.

Food terms also seem to work quite well, with gherkin, sausage or salami for a man. Meat and weapon combinations are also popular for male genitals such as pork sword, beef bayonet or mutton dagger. For women, culinary references include pies, often of the furry or hairy variety such as rabbit. There are various unsavoury references to fish and tuna or the bearded clam. We also have the sweeter honeypot for women.

Sex, Lies and Stereotypes

In the realms of fantasy we have the delicate fairy or the more fearsome hairy Cyclops for a woman. For a man we have 'purple-headed monster', or the 'one-eyed womb weasel'.

If we opt for the pleasure angle we have the 'pink pleasure palace' for a woman, and the 'big red fun bus' for a man.

Assorted offerings for woman include flower, tuppence, poonani, poontang, growler, twat, cooter, box, snatch, flossy, cunt, vadge, snorcher and front bottom. Assorted offerings for men include knob, pecker, plum-tree shaker, cock, bishop, dick, wiener, lad, member, prick, plonker, shaft, inches and veiny bang-stick.

The nonsense approach offers us chuff, quim or coochie for a woman, and diddle, dong or todger for a man. The no-nonsense approach of the anatomy books offers us vagina and penis.

I trust you get the picture.

Not only do we use analogies, metaphors, codes and ciphers to talk about our relationships, we can't even bring ourselves to 'call a spade a spade', or rather call a hoo-hoo a vagina and a wanger a penis. Before we go on to look at some key terms in the real psychology of male and female roles and relationships, I'd like to propose a little exercise to further explore sexual communication.

Exercise: An animated discussion

Imagine that a sexual health organization is producing an animated video. It wants to include two characters based on parts of the body. One is a character based on the vagina and the other is based on the penis. The organization has produced a brief questionnaire in order to formulate the respective personalities for the two characters.

For this exercise you need to consider a number of personality traits and assign them to either the vagina character or the penis character. The traits are:

Aggressive, Decisive, Understanding, Nurturing, Risk-taker, Shy, Affectionate, Strong, Tender, Assertive, Dominating, Independent, Warm, Compassionate

Please write them in the spaces provided on the following page. Don't agonize over it too much, just go with your initial reactions.

Vagina character:

Penis character:

Generally speaking, people tend to allocate personality characteristics according to traditional gender roles. So the vagina character will take on the traits usually associated with the traditional female role, and the penis character will take on the traits associated with the traditional male role. However, we could make the case that traits associated with traditional gender roles are little more than descriptions of our genitals.

In her book *The Apartheid of Sex*, gender and human rights theorist Martine Rothblatt actually refers to women as 'people with vaginas' and refers to men as 'people with penises' to emphasize this link. 'People with vaginas' are described as nurturing, shy, tender, warm, compassionate and understanding. Whereas 'people with penises' are more likely to be described as assertive, aggressive, decisive, risk-taker, strong, dominating and independent-minded.

The names Sineplian and Anigavlian are thinly veiled metaphors, using the words 'penis' and 'vagina' reversed. The whole Sineplian/Anigavlian mythology was used to emphasize the how the 'different planet' approach links genital shape and gender roles.

We carve up human behaviour and experience into two neat categories by viewing the world through 'genitally shaped' filters. A man's experience of the world is supposedly more 'outside' focused; a woman's experience of the world is supposed to be more 'inside' focused. The female gender role is supposed to be about emotions and inner feelings; the male gender role is supposed to be instrumental, with an emphasis on outside goals and achievements.

However, it is not just popular psychology that uses the shapes of genitals to discuss how our personalities are shaped. An eminent psychologist observing children at play reported that boys create exterior-based scenes and build tall towers, while girls create more interior-based domestic scenes. A clear connection is made here between genital shape and the division of labour. The implication is that patterns of play will turn into patterns of work. However, is this an explanation or a justification? Such characterizations are not a million light years away from the power-obsessed Martians or the lovelorn Venusians.

Sex, Lies and Stereotypes

Often, academic psychologists have been criticized for routinely including analyses of gender differences, as if being a man or a woman was just another personality trait. Psychology is often viewed as being objective and apolitical. But is it political to refuse to acknowledge the social, economic and political conditions that have shaped and enforced traditional gender roles? Women traditionally stayed at home and men went out to work because that's how the labour was divided.

The neurologist and psychotherapist Sigmund Freud (1856–1939), among others, talked about our anatomy being our destiny. Biologists and evolutionary psychologists echo similar sentiments. It is clear that the 'different planet' approach is just another way of saying that our destiny is inexorably fixed at birth by the shape of our genitals. However, is this a model for our lives that we wish to perpetuate? Is the solution to our problems to play-act the roles of Mr Penis and Miss Vagina? Alternatively, isn't it time we put away our willies and winkies, our Marys and minkies, our Sineplians and Anigavlians? Instead, don't we need to raise our level of awareness by looking at some key concepts, definitions and arguments around the subjects of the roles of men and women and human relationships?

What's the difference? War of the words

Amid scandal at the highest level in the United States government, the whole world was gripped by the question as to exactly what constituted 'sexual relations'. In short, 'what is sex?'. Initially the question took us by surprise. However, it wasn't long before people were saying: 'Well, that all depends on what you mean by sex.' So firstly, we will attempt to define exactly what we mean by sex.

Another word that frequently crops up in discussions of relationships is gender. Although the words sex and gender are used interchangeably, they are not the same thing.

Sex

Sex has two definitions. First, we'll talk about sex in terms of behaviour, as in sexual acts. Second, we'll talk about sex as an identity, as a biological status. In biological (identity) terms, we have two main categories of sex: male and female. Our genitals, chromosomes, genes and internal reproductive systems identify us as a particular sex. All of these act as partial definitions of sex, although our genitals are often used as the central characteristic. We also use the word sex to refer to various acts we perform, usually with others, and most often with our genitals. We all have slightly different views about what constitutes sex but the largest degree of agreement is that sex equals penile penetration of the vagina or vaginal engulfment of the penis.

A recent survey revealed just what Americans thought constituted sexual relations. Presented with various descriptions of sexual behaviour they were asked which of them constituted having 'had sex'. Three out of five people (59 per cent) said that oral-genital contact did not constitute having 'had sex'. One in five people (19 per cent) said that anal sex did not constitute having 'had sex'. So, it seems that when someone (heterosexual) says 'I had sex last night', we most likely assume that it was penis-vagina intercourse. The emphasis is very much on heterosexuality as the benchmark. By focusing on the penis and vagina we emphasize sex for reproduction, that is procreation over recreation.

A sexual script in academic literature refers to the usual sequence in which sexual acts occur. Men and women tend to agree on a recognizable sequence of behaviours:

> kissing, caressing, manual stimulation of genitals, oral stimulation of genitals and finally penis-vagina intercourse

However, differences occur in ratings given by women and men of the arousal levels gained in each stage in the sequence. For men, the arousal increases with each step peaking with penetration. In contrast, women's evaluations of arousal peak prior to penetration and actually dip for intercourse. We will consider this point in greater detail when we come to look at human anatomy in chapter 4. Penetration is also not necessarily imperative to homosexual male sexuality. Various surveys report anal sex is a central activity for only about 7 in 10 gay men.

Gender

Where sex as an identity is rooted in biology, gender has its roots in culture. Gender refers to the social and cultural aspects associated with biological sex (as an identity). Our assigned gender is the label given to us by others, usually at birth. The categorization is based on the more visible penis. Thus the presence of a penis means 'It's a boy', whereas the absence of a penis means 'It's a girl'. This wording is deliberate and I will elaborate on this in subsequent chapters. Being labelled a boy or a girl sets up expectations in terms of how we behave socially and culturally. These patterns of expectation are our gender roles (sometimes referred to as sex roles). It is important to note that gender roles may differ between different cultures at any given point in time. They may also change over time within the same culture. So although anatomy (sex) is relatively constant, gender may vary.

Gender identity refers to the pattern of expectations with which a person, that is a girl or a boy, identifies. Children become aware of their own gender identity around two-and-a-half to three years, but it may be as early as 18 months. However, this still may entertain the idea that it is possible to cross over and change gender. It is not until around the ages of six to seven that children grasp the idea that gender is a constant. At this time they are said to acquire gender constancy, as they grasp the idea that girls eventually become women and boys become men. Children may get the idea of gender constancy earlier if they become aware of the differences between girls' and boys' genitals.

Gender roles are very much about distinct patterns of behaviour. These include the way we dress, mannerisms, our voices and so on. It is an elaborate system of cues that tell other people what gender we are. Gender is not so much about understanding who you are, but how you should fit in. Many gender theorists argue that gender is really a process or a performance rather than a fixed identity. It is something we do rather than something we are. Gender is about keeping up appearances. If we play the gender game according to the rules, then we can expect to be correctly identified as a man or a woman.

Gender-role stereotypes

Gender-role stereotypes refer to rigid role-expectations. Whenever we use the word 'stereotypical' it is usually to convey that something is predictable and typical. It's a word that comes from Greek and roughly translates as, 'fixed impression' and originally referred to a method of duplicate printing. This conveys the sense of producing many identical copies. Stereotypes in the modern-day sense are little packets of knowledge that contain generalizations about something, most often about types of people. So, whenever we use the phrase 'typical man' or 'typical woman', what we are really saying is 'stereotypical man' or 'stereotypical woman'. The same applies when we refer to 'real men' or 'real women'. When we assume that something is typical of all members of a group, we are over-generalizing.

When we are talking about gender stereotypes, these include a range of characteristics about what it means to be 'male' or 'female, 'masculine' or 'feminine'. These may include physical characteristics, attitudes regarding 'typical' behaviours, personality traits and the respective roles men and women are supposed to play in society. Although it appears to be merely descriptive, it is *actually* prescriptive. Stereotypes don't describe; they dictate. They often contain many 'oughts', 'shoulds' and 'musts'. Stereotypes function to keep clear boundaries between men and women.

The links between sexuality and gender are discussed further throughout chapter 10, here I want to highlight a key link between sexual behaviour and gender identity, namely: how the way in which we have sex is linked to gender roles. Traditionally (synonymous with 'stereotypically') men have been the ones to take the initiative in sex. If we equate 'normal' sex with the missionary position, the man goes on top. The male is viewed as more active because he does the penetration (the work). A woman is viewed as more passive, in that sex is something done to her rather than by her. These stereotypes have found their way into the way we view lesbian and gay relationships. Erroneously, people may assume that one partner plays the male role while the other plays the female role. Some gay and lesbian people may indeed embrace these roles, but many do not. Lesbian and gay relationships are much more likely to be based on a partnership model and in these relationships gender and how partners have sex are not necessarily related.

Now that we have discussed the dynamics and relationships within sex, sexuality and gender, let's return to *The Great Divide* to spot some of the black holes in the mythology.

BLACK HOLES

The Great Divide mythology is simply an account of gender stereotypes. The same is true of the 'different planet' approach. Every time we use the phrase 'opposite sex' we buy into the idea that men and women are fundamentally separated by some great divide.

Common to *The Great Divide* and the 'different planet' approach is the idea of communicating by means of analogies and metaphors. However, at a certain point we need to let the analogy go. Analogies and metaphors are meant to introduce real world concepts not replace them. It's a basic building block of human learning to link ideas and concepts together. We learn by association. So, perhaps it's not surprising that with constant repetition and switching back and forth, the metaphorical terms and the real world terms become interchangeable. So when I talk to you about Anigavlians (or Venusians) you interpret this as me talking about women. Similarly, if I talk about Sineplians (or Martians) you translate this into 'men'. This means that a discussion about relationships no longer has to be supported by real evidence from the real world. The fantasy world anecdote is surrogate evidence.

Put simply, the evidence doesn't have to get in the way of a good story. When the world of fact and fiction become amalgamated we tend to overlook any inconsistencies. For instance, how on earth do people stuck on opposite sides of the Great Divide go about the serious business (and pleasure) of making babies? Let's examine this fundamental black hole.

All Sineplians have the same type of genitals: penises. All Anigavlians have the same type of genitals: vaginas. So how do they reproduce? The Sineplians, being more technologically advanced, have probably perfected cloning. Unfortunately the Anigavlians, being less scientifically minded, probably made babies out of papier-mâché and raffia. Or else the Sineplians abandoned the incomplete Sineplian babies (without penises) and the kindly Anigavlians rescued and raised them.

Now, if you think they have problems coming from opposite sides of a canyon, such problems pale into insignificance when the two races come from different planets. long-distance relationships are one thing, but that's just ridiculous.

Let's consider the division of labour and the provision of childcare. While all the Sineplians are out at their laboratories, who's looking after the kids? Maybe a case can be made for progressive attitudes to gay parenting. Maybe Sineplians have invented robots to do it, or maybe they sneak a few Anigavlians across to look after the children. This may work with people separated by a canyon, but what about if they are separated by lght years? By far the most logical thing to do would be for the Sineplians to colonize Anigavlia, which is exactly what they did.

But how did thousands of years of inter-species breeding achieve nothing in bringing the two species closer together? All they seem to have in common is amnesia. Surely, the differences should have disappeared over successive generations? They retain an illusory perpetual difference because Anigavlian/Venusian simply means person with a vagina. Sineplian/Martian means person with a penis. For the metaphor to work we have to live in the fairytale land of birds and bees, storks and gooseberry bushes. Surely, if they are compatible at a reproductive level, then they must be very similar biologically?

In justifying different abilities based on different bodies, the different planet approach obscures power differences and social inequalities. For instance, can *The Great Divide* approach explain why women get paid less than men for doing the same job? Is it because women's hands aren't as big as men's hands and therefore they need less money to fill them? The subtext of the 'different planet' approach is clearly about power and submission.

Conclusion: Abyss-ness as usual?

Gender is often seen as a fundamental unit of identity whereas, more often, it is really a performance. Rather than something we are, our gender identity is more like the role associated with an actor who has become typecast. Or rather, in the case of gender, we have become 'stereotype-cast'. We are expected to play certain roles. Gender-role stereotypes create the impression that men and women stand on opposite sides of an abyss that cannot (or rather should not) be traversed. Gender-role stereotypes embody a whole ideology; a systematic interrelated set of beliefs from which we find it difficult to escape. Appropriate gender roles fit in with our concepts of normality and decency, which all help to maintain a cohesive view of the world. Without such values we assume that our world would plunge into oblivion. Nevertheless, Western societies have still made giant steps in narrowing the gender gap, that is, reducing social inequality based on biological sex.

In this chapter we have really focused on two filters by which we view the roles of men and women. Firstly we have looked at the biological filter that makes us view gender through genital-shaped filters. Secondly we have begun to address the societal and cultural power differences and considered that gender is often viewed from a male perspective.

So, with possible oblivion staring us in the face, we need to explore what is at the heart of our need for simple structure. What is the attraction of gender roles based on genital shape? In the next chapter we will explore the dynamics of black-and-white thinking and why we find it so compelling.

2

Why Do We View the World the Way We Do?

To be, or not to be. That is the question.
— William Shakespeare, English playwright (1564–1616)

There are two types of people. Those who come into a room and say, "Well, here I am!" and those who come in and say, "Ah, there you are." — Frederick L. Collins, modern-day American politician

There are two kinds of people in this world: those who believe the world can be divided into two kinds of people, and those who don't — Benchley's Law of Distinction, Robert Benchley (1889–1945)

PREVIEW

In this chapter we will:

* Explore different ways of viewing the world with a short quiz.
* Consider information from a range of sources to explore why we are attracted to black-and-white (binary) categories to view the world, both at a cultural and an individual level.
* Consider the impact of holding or using such narrow viewpoints.

Points of view

We often talk about being on the same wavelength as other people. We use phrases such as 'speaking my language' or 'singing from the same hymn sheet'. We may even talk about 'common ground', 'pulling in the same direction', 'sharing the same vision', or 'seeing eye to eye'. However, when we are 'at odds' or 'at loggerheads' with someone we may facetiously ask them: 'And just what planet are you from?'. Sometimes we may accuse people of being closed minded if they aren't receptive to our point of view. Hopefully our different views won't cause us to 'come to blows' or 'be at each other's throats' with 'daggers drawn'. Despite our differences, we all share a fond-

QUIZ: WAYS OF VIEWING THE WORLD

1. _____ I like to do jobs where the instructions are clear.
2. _____ The idea of living in a different country for a while appeals to me.
3. _____ I enjoy the excitement of being in uncertain or unpredictable situations.
4. _____ It's not possible to accurately describe a person using a few words or categories.
5. _____ I prefer parties where I know most of the people rather than those where most of the people are new to me.
6. _____ I cope well with change and find it easy to adapt.
7. _____ I prefer to read things that support my values and view of the world.
8. _____ In the long run, it's possible to get more done by tackling small, simple problems than by tackling large complicated ones.
9. _____ Different and original people are often the most interesting and stimulating.
10. _____ Some problems just don't have a solution.
11. _____ I prefer to stick with what I'm used to rather than trying something unfamiliar.
12. _____ People who insist on straight yes or no answers often don't realize how complex things are.
13. _____ The sooner we universally adopt similar values and ideas, the better.
14. _____ A regular routine with few unexpected happenings or disruptions is something to be thankful for.
15. _____ Most important decisions are based on insufficient information.

Sex, Lies and Stereotypes

ness for communicating using images, metaphors and analogies.

In this chapter we are going to explore the idea of perceptual filters in greater detail. We are also going to look at the concept of attitudes and how they help us make sense of the world. However, before we consider the differences and similarities in the ways people view the world, I invite you to do the quiz below.

The aim of the quiz is to get you to consider the way you view the world. It is about showing greater insight of your own personal perceptual filters. As such, there are no right or wrong answers. It is your own personal view that counts. Don't agonize too much over each question, just read them through and go with your gut reaction, as this is often a more

16. _____ Having clearly defined roles in life, which people stick to, helps us all get along better.

17. _____ Open-ended tasks and assignments give people opportunity to show initiative and originality.

18. _____ Experts who don't come up with a definite answer, probably don't know very much.

19. _____ It's not possible to predict how people will react from one situation to another.

20. _____ People who live well-ordered lives according to a regular schedule probably miss most of the joy of living.

21. _____ A good teacher is one who makes you wonder about your way of looking at things.

22. _____ I like to have a place for everything and everything in its place.

23. _____ It's more fun to tackle a complex problem rather than to solve a simple one.

24. _____ I don't mind having to change my plans at the last minute.

25. _____ I get frustrated being with people who are spontaneous and impulsive.

26. _____ When I meet people, I look for one basic characteristic through which I try to understand them.

27. _____ I prefer to seek out information and experiences that challenge my way of looking at the world.

28. _____ I become anxious when the rules are not clear.

29. _____ People who are different and unusual are really just being difficult.

30. _____ The personality we are born with is the same as the one we die with.

accurate reflection of how you really feel about things. There are 30 statements. All you need to do is indicate your level of agreement using the following scale:

0 points = *Agree strongly*
1 point = *Agree mostly*
2 points = *Agree slightly*
3 points = *Disagree slightly*
4 points = *Disagree mostly*
5 points = *Disagree strongly*

Write your response next to each of the statements (using *whole* points only), and please answer ALL statements.

SCORING

To find out your score you will need to do a few simple calculations.

Score A = Your scores from the following questions:
   q2 + q3 + q4 + q6 + q9 + q10 + q12 + q15 + q17 + q19 + q20 + q21 + q23 + q24 + q27
You should get a number from 0 to 75. If you haven't, check your calculations.

Score B = 75 - Score A
Again, Score B should be a number between 0 and 75. If it isn't then you need to go back and check your calculations.

Score C = Your scores from the following questions:
   q1 + q5 +q7 + q8 + q11 +q13 + q14 + q16 + q18 + q22 + q25 + q26 + q28 + q29 + q30

Total Score = Score B + Score C _____

What your score indicates

Scores from **0 to 50** are considered to be **LOW**
Scores from **51 to 100** are considered to be **MODERATE**
Scores from **101 to 150** are considered to be **HIGH**

Sex, Lies and Stereotypes

Before we look at what the scores indicate I'd just like to say that, although it is based on a number of serious academic sources, the quiz is only meant to provide an indication of how people *tend* to behave. It's offered for information purposes only and should not be interpreted as any form of diagnosis. I certainly don't expect to see high scorers or low scorers handing out leaflets, trying to recruit members in the shopping mall.

Low scorers

Low scorers tend to live their lives according to a minimal structure, and actually seem to thrive (or are at least comfortable) in times of change and uncertainty. They enjoy a challenge. When faced with a task, they may prefer to explore options rather than stick to fixed instructions.

Low scorers are people who don't need to find absolute (yes/no) answers. They can entertain a whole spectrum of possibility. They may become irritated with people whom they consider to be overly orderly. Low scorers tend to focus on the individuality (complexity) of people, rather than trying to fit people into narrow categories. They tend to shy away from clearly defined labels and roles and resent being pigeon-holed.

The 'different planet' approach to gender and relationships is unlikely to appeal to low scorers. They like to push the boundaries. They may be perceived by others as different and unusual, and may be drawn to the same types of people. Low scorers may be people who enjoy spontaneity and who show flexibility and are happy to 'go with the flow'. They are unlikely to enjoy having to stick to a rigid routine.

Some people may perceive low scorers as very exciting people, while to others they seem plain reckless. Low scorers may be viewed as lacking direction or discipline and seem as though they just leave everything to chance. To very high scorers, they are viewed as difficult and uncooperative. For scores of less than 25, these tendencies may be more pronounced. Conversely, for scores of 25 to 50, these tendencies appear more moderate.

High scorers

High scorers are people who tend to need a high degree of structure in their lives. They tend to be uncomfortable (or even become anxious) with vague or uncertain situations. They favour well-organized routines and systems. High scorers often prefer to work to clearly defined guidelines, procedures and instructions. They prefer familiarity to novelty, tending to stick with what they know. They tend not to cope well with change, dislike having to alter their plans at the last minute and dislike people whom they perceive to be impulsive and spontaneous, different or unusual.

High scorers tend to be people who are most comfortable with others who share their world-view. This may make it difficult for them to consider opposing views. They are often perceived as 'jumping to conclusions'. High scorers have a tendency to use simple (black-and-white) categories to structure the world.

The 'different planet' approach may seem quite appealing to high scorers because they prefer clearly defined roles and boundaries. They have a tendency to view personality as consistent, predictable and constant. High scorers may think the world would be a better place if we all adopted the same values (as long it was their values). High scorers often appear 'set in their ways' and from a low scorer's perspective they may be viewed as rigid, inflexible or even intolerant. They may also be perceived as stubborn, narrow-minded or dogmatic.

For scores from 101 to 125, these tendencies may be more moderate. However, for scores of over 125, these tendencies appear more pronounced.

Moderate scorers

Moderate scorers are by far the most difficult to describe. A score in the mid-range indicates that such people have a degree of flexibility in the way they view the world. Moderate scorers may need more certainty in some areas of their lives than they do in others. So, instead of showing a strong tendency to behave in a particular way, moderate scorers are more likely to respond to the demands of a particular situation; considering all the possibilities. As with low and high scorers, there is a degree of variability among people who score in this range.

Scores of 67 to 84 represent the middle of the whole range of scores. Low-moderate scores range from 51 to 66, and high–moderate scores range from 85 to 100. Moderate scorers often appear to take the middle course and they may be perceived as bland. Yet in many ways they are more unpredictable than consistently unpredictable people.

Although the quiz produces a whole spectrum of scores from 0 to 150, it is simpler to divide scores into three main categories. However, even then, it is much easier to describe the two extremes (low and high scorers) than to describe those in the middle range. Extreme groups are more likely to respond at the opposite ends of the scale and therefore show more consistent patterns of response. It is easier to assume all the responses form a neat straight line. A closer inspection of the scores may yield more of a zigzag pattern.

By far the best course of action would be to describe each score individually. However, this would need another book. Trying to describe the subtle difference would be almost impossible. At some point, patterns only emerge if we look at little pockets of scores. We are faced with this same dilemma constantly. The world is a complicated place. We cannot process all the information that comes our way, so we need to simplify it.

Your score is offered merely to indicate a tendency you may have when attempting to structure (make sense of) your experiences. Some people will think it describes them pretty well and others will not. We will pick up the discussion of the quiz later on in this chapter. Meanwhile, let's consider in more depth our psychological need for structure.

Attitudes

A woman was walking down the road when suddenly her hat blew off. It landed at the feet of a man walking in the opposite direction with his dog. The dog seized the hat and chewed it up into little pieces. The woman shouted furiously: 'Your dog has ruined my hat.' To her surprise the man replied: 'Don't worry you can get another one.' Taken aback the woman snapped: 'I don't like your attitude', to which the man replied: 'It wasn't my 'at he chewed, it was yours.'

The term 'attitude' has become part of our everyday language. We talk about people having a bad attitude or giving us attitude. We are also stopped on the street by market researchers who are eager to find out our attitudes on a range of behaviours and products. People even telephone us when we are half way through a meal to find out our attitudes. We are encouraged to call premium-rate numbers during chat shows and magazine programmes for the privilege of letting the programme makers know our attitudes. It's not only money that makes the world go round, attitudes do, too. We've got them and sometimes we express them freely, sometimes we don't and sometimes we dare not.

At the simplest level, attitudes are our likes and dislikes. Attitudes are a learned outlook towards people, things or situations. We can have attitudes towards just about anything. The word attitude comes from Latin and means 'fit and ready for action'. In ancient times it meant 'readiness', as in 'athletes ready to compete'. However, we can use this definition and apply it to a mental state of readiness, one for processing information. Attitudes are the 'get ready and steady' before the 'go'. Attitudes serve a number of functions for us.

The function I'm going to focus on in this chapter is the knowledge function. Attitudes provide a frame of reference to help us organize our perceptions and beliefs. They help provide us with stability and consistency of meaning in the real world. Personal experience helps shape our attitudes but we 'inherit' a host of ready-made attitudes in the form of cultural norms, such as the appropriate roles for males and females. Just like the athlete on the starting block, we sometimes 'jump the gun'. Sometimes we don't make judgements based on all of the information: we pre-judge. The tendency to pre-judge is the literal meaning of an extreme form of attitude: prejudice. Much psychological research carried out after the Second World War (1939–45) focused on the links between prejudice and personalities. From early theories aimed at explaining political extremism, general theories then emerged. They highlighted the human need to organize our environment using simple mental methods and categories.

Human processes of attention and perception rely on filters to screen out irrelevant information. We are like cognitive cherry pickers – collecting information with the most cultural and personal relevance and rejecting everything else. This is how we make sense of the world. Some people have a much greater need to structure their environment than others. For these people, any failure to satisfy this need for structure may actually provoke anxiety. So when an individual encounters something unfamiliar – like some situation or some person that cannot be easily 'processed' (placed) into pre-defined, simple categories – they feel discomfort. In simple terms, if something makes us uncomfortable, then we are more likely to have a negative attitude towards it. So it can be argued that the tendency to pre-judge negatively is at least in part a function of the way we process information.

IN THE BEGINNING

As with computer software, our inherited ready-made attitudes and cultural norms help us process information. Admittedly, the software gets

Sex, Lies and Stereotypes

revised over time as our personal experience adds or subtracts a bit of code here or there. However, in essence we are all still using the same operating system. We are now up to 'FILTERS 21C'. We made dramatic changes to 'FILTERS 20C', especially in how we viewed the roles of women and men. However I'm more interested in the earliest forms of software – 'FILTERS BC' or rather 'APPLE BC' and the point at which we gained the knowledge of good and evil in the Garden of Eden. For it is religious texts that provide us with the earliest accounts of how humans attempted to make sense of the world. Such accounts attempted to explain how the universe came about and, most importantly, the roles (including gender roles) and functions of a particular culture's inhabitants and their relationship to outsiders ('one of us' or 'one of them'). The importance of these accounts should not be underestimated. The influence of religious accounts can still be seen in aspects of psychology, psychiatry, medicine and law. However, the most noticeable influence is in the way in which Western cultures organize and structure matters of gender and sexuality.

We can make a broad distinction between two types of religion. There are those that worship one god, such as Christianity, Judaism and Islam, and those religions that worship more than one god, such as Hinduism and the religion of ancient Egypt. These two types of belief system have fundamental differences in the way they structure the world. One-god religions tend to organize the world according to black-and-white categories; there are rigid boundaries between moral and divine realms; there are also rigid boundaries between the function and roles of people, including gender roles. The one-god is male. In stark contrast, multiple-god religions tend to include female gods. There are less-rigid boundaries between mortal and divine realms. In fact, the gods and mortals sometimes have sexual intercourse. Some gods may possess both male and female characteristics. In modern day terminology, they are hermaphrodites.

Now, when we compare the attitudes to sex between one-god and multiple-god religions, there is a distinct difference. Looking back to ancient Egyptian and Canaanite religions, we see that sex was used as part of some sacred rituals – something that irked the ancient Israelites to say the least. In Western cultures, we have inherited attitudes to sex that are more negative. Sex is viewed as something that is in need of control or regulation. The software we have inherited from our one-god universe led us to form ideas as to how sex, sexuality and gender are organized in everyday life. So in one-god cultures, sex and gender are based on a binary (two-option) system: you are either male or female, and they are classed as opposites. Sexuality is also (reluctantly) based on the two-option system of 'straight' or 'gay'. The system does not allow for anomalies. Glitches in the system tend to be avoided, at best tolerated, rather than accepted.

In contrast, a multiple-god system allows for both a more relaxed approach to gender roles and for degrees of ambiguity. The boundaries are fuzzy so it is easier to accommodate difference. One-god religions are often antagonistic to the beliefs of others. It is no coincidence that many of the things we consider to be occult practices have their origins in other religions. Horror films involving mummies and evil gods have tainted our view of ancient Egypt. We use the word 'philistine' to refer to someone who is hostile or indifferent to culture. The word has the same roots as 'Palestine'. The fact that the Philistines were more cultured than their enemies is of little relevance. They were considered uncultured by their one-god worshipping enemies simply because they did not share the same world-view. For one-god religions the integrity of boundaries is paramount. One-god cultures organize experience in this way: the world is carved up into categories of good/evil, sacred/profane, us/them and zeroes/ones. That's just how it is.

Exercise: Zeroes and ones

The exercise on the opposite page is inspired by an idea in Kate Bornstein's *My Gender Workbook*. I have adapted it to incorporate the themes in this book. For each of the pairs of items, circle one that applies most to you or your life. You may also want to cross out the ones that bear no relation to you or the way you live your life. Please do the exercise now.

You no doubt found it easy to respond to some of these. Others may have proved more difficult. Either they didn't apply at all or else you wanted a kind of halfway option. Some of them might fit in very well with your sense of identity. Others will be quite alien to you. They are all very simple categorizations.

The main functions of early religious accounts were to help people forge a sense of collective identity (in a hostile environment) and to make sense of a complex world. Unfortunately, there are rarely discrete, perfectly self-contained categories in the natural (real) world. In order to make things easier to comprehend and process, we create some manageable meaningful chunks. We use language to create categories and boundaries but problematically the distinctions and cut-off points are arbitrary as there

Exercise: Zeroes and ones

Male/Female	Active/Passive	Young/Old	Rich/Poor
Good/Bad	Masculine/Feminine	Giver/Taker	Straight/Gay
Butch/Femme	One of us/One of them	Beautiful/Ugly	Happy/Sad
Fat/Thin	Blue eyes/Brown eyes	Public/Private	AC/DC
Nice/Nasty	Carnivore/Herbivore	Survivor/Victim	Mr/Mrs
Short/Tall	Material/Spiritual	Town/Country	Country/Western
Up/Down	Natural/Unnatural	Sacred/Profane	Urban/Rural
Right/Wrong	Home/Career	Black/White	Venus/Mars
Penis/Vagina	Brother/Sister	Mother/Father	Arthur/Martha
Cat/Dog	Other half/Better half	Lucky/Unlucky	Penis/Anus
Ms/Mr	Gendered/Transgendered	Work/Play	Tea/Coffee
Soaps/Opera	Hard sums/Colouring in	Pink/Blue	Towers/Flowers
Tragedy/Comedy	B&W/Technicolor	Smoker/Breather	Top/Bottom
Tough/Tender	Powerful/Powerless	Strong/Weak	Positive/Negative
Healthy/Sick	Sineplian/Anigavlian	Sadist/Masochist	Clitoris/Penis
Stud/Slag	Normal/Abnormal	Virgin/Whore	Zero/One

And finally: All of the above/None of the above

aren't any clear-cut boundaries; sometimes they are fuzzy or blurred. In Western cultures our most preferred classification tends to be binary. That's the two-option, either/or, zero and one based language at the heart of computer programming. So we create a kind of black-and-white, all-or-nothing view of the world.

Looking back at your answers to the previous exercise, did you circle 'zero' or 'one'? Looking at some of the pairs, both options are roughly equivalent. However, with others there is a sense of value judgement, either overtly or covertly, explicitly or implicitly. Performance artist Laurie Anderson says in her piece *Zeroes and Ones*: 'Everybody wants to be number one, and no one wants to be a nothing.'

Whenever we are offered two options, inevitably we make comparisons. Comparison leads to judgement: that one option is better than the other. In the last chapter I briefly touched on the subject of power differences. Power differences often creep into black-and-white binary thinking. Kate Bornstein addresses the concept of power in the search for the 'perfect gender', the standard by which all else is measured. In agreement with many critical theorists she addresses the biases in our power structure. The usual list is given, which includes white, male, heterosexual, middle-class, Protestant and so on. However, she also cites binary thinking and linear thinking. It is not clear why black-and-white binary thinking should be connected with power until we look at the basic laws at arriving at binary categories. Binary thinking, common to Western culture is organized around three basic laws:

1. **The law of identity**, which states: *Whatever is, is.*
2. **The law of contradiction**, which states: *Nothing can both be and not be.*
3. **The law of excluded middle**, which states: *Everything must either be or not be.*

No doubt you can think of a fourth law: *Thou shalt state the bloody obvious.* Common to all of these laws is the need to reduce ambiguity or uncertainty. They all attempt to get rid of the grey areas. This is especially true of the third law – just look at its name. However if we look at the law of excluded middle, we see how the power imbalance creeps in. First of all, it's surprisingly similar to Shakespeare's 'To be or not to be'. Let's slightly re-word it to make the point clearer: 'To be something or not to be something'; 'To be someone or not to be someone'.

To be represents **something**	**Not to be** represents **nothing**
Something is represented by **one**	**Nothing** is represented by **zero**
Presence = 1	**Absence = 0**

One item in the pair has the leading role: it forms the basis of definition. To make this abstract point a little more concrete just look through a few magazines. They are full of tall, thin attractive people. Standards are defined by tall not short, by thin not fat and by attractive not unattractive. If you are tall you get one point, if you are not you get zero. If you are thin you get one point, if you are not you get zero. If you are attractive you get one point, if you are not you get zero. It may not be fair but it is there. One side 'counts' more than the other. One side is valued more highly.

Rather contentiously I argued in the last chapter that the assignment of gender is based on the presence of a penis. The main reason being that the penis is more visible. So let's apply the law of excluded middle to this process. If a penis is present then it's a boy; if it is absent then it's not a boy. Let's translate this into the zeroes and ones of the computer binary system.

If you have one then you are number one. The number '1' even looks like a one – we're talking unsophisticated genital symbolism here. The '0' looks like the opposite of having one. Gender is defined from a male perspective, so the one comes before the zero. Central to the female gender-role stereotype is that women put the feelings of others before their own.

In some areas of China, gay men's roles are often characterized by zeroes and ones. The active partner (the top) is referred to as the one, whereas the passive partner (the bottom) is referred to as the zero. The 'one' (penis) has higher status than the 'zero' (hole). This shows that whenever we encounter binary options of any real social significance, there is always a power imbalance. This power imbalance is compounded because we never consider binary categories in isolation; we always string them together and assume that they all line up, like tall, thin and attractive. We saw this process in the categories created for the Zeroes and Ones exercise on page 41. If we look at the extreme ends of a continuum, it is easier to see the values all forming a neat straight line. So, let's look at the string of values for gender-role stereotypes:

One = Penis = Man = Masculine = Active = Tough = Independent
Zero = Vagina = Woman = Feminine = Passive = Tender = Dependent

Considering the definition of the word 'vagina' can illuminate this further. It literally means 'a sheath for a sword'. Do the penis and vagina sound like equal partners? Clearly the penis has the leading role while the vagina has a supporting role.

We can also use the law of excluded middle to explain negative attitudes to gay men. Masculinity and heterosexuality are intimately entwined. *To be* a real man you are supposed to have sex with women. *Not to be* 'straight' means you can't be a real man. You can see how the binary values line up. However, a gay man is biologically male. What we see is that gay men break the law of excluded middle. Gay men fall into a kind of 'no man's land'. From this perspective we can see that deviation from sexual norms is partly a deviation from gender norms. People who cannot be easily classified may be seen as an obstacle to a harmonious society. I'm sure I don't need to list the various groups of people who have at some time or another been viewed as outsiders. It's enough to say that the list is based on gender, religious, ethnic, political or lifestyle differences. They all represent a challenge to the dominant values. They stray from the 'straight and narrow' of Normsville (not pleasant at all).

So we can see that negative attitudes are in part a function of the way we structure the world. We attempt to process information using simple (two-option) binary categories. However, it is inevitable, given the complexity of the world, that these simple laws of classification are often broken. We also need to consider the power biases inherent in these simple categories. Invariably one item in a binary pair is privileged over the other. So having looked at the social and cultural basis ('operating system') for black-and-white thinking, let's consider the impact of individual differences.

I USED TO BE UNCERTAIN, BUT NOW I'M NOT SURE

Black-and-white categorization addresses a social and cultural need. However, as we cannot escape culture, it also addresses individual needs that vary from person to person. According to psychologist Erik Erikson, the human need to carve up the world into binary categories begins in childhood with the concepts of 'public and private' and 'clean and dirty'. Around the time of toilet training, the child begins to question boundaries, mainly where the self ends and others begin. She or he starts to work out the 'me' from the 'not-me'. The child also starts to learn that some parts of the body are private and thus must remain hidden. It is really at this time that the child learns a capacity for self-control and a sense of independence and autonomy, or else feelings of self-doubt and shame. Other research has suggested that the categorization of good/bad body parts forms the basis of classifying good/bad people.

But we can't talk about toilet training unless we mention Sigmund Freud, albeit briefly. It is a common expression to call people 'anally retentive' if they are a bit 'uptight'. This refers to Freud's idea of the anal stage of psycho-sexual development. Put simply, Freud argued that a child gains pleasure and control of an interaction by holding onto its faeces. When the child grows up he or she retains an anal fixation, which results in him or her being rather miserly and stubborn with a strong need for order in their lives.

Less fancifully, one of the main themes that emerged from research into personality types and the tendency to pre-judge was the concept of intolerance of ambiguity. This brings us back to the exercise on pages 32–3. Some people seem to be able to cope with ambiguity or uncertainty more easily or more readily than others. People with a greater intolerance of ambiguity (uncertainty) have a greater need to apply rigid categories. People who show a greater tolerance of ambiguity (uncertainty) tend to be more flexible when it comes to applying categories. Research has shown that people show similar patterns of attitudes across different contexts.

People who tend to hold very status-conscious, power-based rigid authoritarian values within the family, tend to hold similar views in other relationships and towards social and political issues. People who are intolerant of ambiguity or uncertainty tend to be more conventional and more authoritarian – and so they tend to favour censorship. They also tend towards more traditional gender roles. People more tolerant of uncertainty and ambiguity tend to be more liberal in their views.

Intolerance of ambiguity or uncertainty also indicates a tendency to view human beings as similar and find it difficult to take into account cultural or individual differences. This may lead to a greater tendency to apply stereotypes when faced with ambiguous behaviour, as a way of 'filling in the gaps'. By contrast, a person with a greater degree of tolerance for ambiguity or uncertainty is more likely to be receptive to new ideas and look at things from different perspectives. Ambiguity intolerance is also associated with religious beliefs that are more dogmatic. Difficulties with ambiguity or uncertainty can also mean difficulty with intimacy.

Being intolerant of ambiguity, which may cause anxiety, means such people tend to pre-judge because of insufficient information. They may over-generalize or 'jump the gun' to arrive at premature and erroneous conclusions. Complex or novel situations result in a knee-jerk reaction and people play it safe or 'go with what they know'. Whereas people who are more tolerant of uncertainty and ambiguity seem more predisposed to 'go with the flow'. We can see that intolerance of ambiguity operates very much on a situational level, suggesting that it is more amenable to change. It is very much about trying to break out of a comfort zone.

We are more likely to pre-judge if we use categories for structuring the world that are overly simplistic. What we discover is that people who pre-judge demand or use a more clear-cut structure to organize their world-view, albeit a narrow and inadequate one. Such people tend to cling to tried-and-tested habits when a radical or novel solution to a problem would be more effective. Whenever possible they latch onto what is simple, safe and definite. Grey-toned reality is overlooked in favour of the simpler black-and-white.

Returning to the exercise on pages 32–3, we are presented with two extremes. There are those who demand a rigid black-and-white structure to the world, and those who don't seem to require any structure at all. However, it is not a black-and-white picture. Many people tend to fall into the many shades of grey in between. No matter where you are in the continuum, the most important thing is to ask yourself how you feel about your score. Does it reflect your tendencies when trying to structure your world? Does your style or tendency help you or hinder you? Are you too rigid or are you too flexible? The interpretation is very much with you. Do you need a more balanced view of the world? If so, you either have to lighten up or tighten up. Simply review some of the questions from the Ways of Viewing the World quiz on pages 32–3 and consider the implications in responding in the opposite way. For the high scorers this may mean challenging order, routine and predictability. For low scorers it may mean imposing more structure, discipline and focus. As for the moderate scorers, they are free to swing both ways.

Conclusion: To be or not to be

The need to create an orderly world with governable rules is central and necessary to the human condition. We have discussed how the use of binary (black-and-white) thinking is part of our cultural software. Our own personal software either reduces or exaggerates the extent of this cultural inheritance. We are culturally drawn to simple categories that explain the function of attitudes as labour-saving devices. Categories simplify and structure the mass of complex information impinging upon us. Therefore, we find any account that provides a ready-made structure of the world attractive. This is true also of one that supports our pre-programmed tendencies to seek simplicity (at the expense of accuracy). Binary thinking or 'the lure of the black-and-white view' is a fundamental filter we use whenever we consider gender roles and sexuality.

In the next chapter we address the untenable nature of gender stereotypes and consider how we often live our lives in the shadows of these ideals, negotiating the fuzzy boundaries of grey-toned reality.

3

Gender Stereotypes, Grey Areas and Fuzzy Boundaries

There is nothing worse than a sharp image of a fuzzy concept – Ansel Adams, photographer (1902–84)

In times of change the learners will inherit the earth, while the learned will find themselves beautifully equipped to deal with a world that no longer exists
– Eric Hoffer, philosopher (1902–83)

PREVIEW

In this chapter we will:

* Consider the expectations of gender-role stereotypes and the tenability of being 'real men' and 'real women'.
* Briefly discuss the factors that help shape gender roles.
* Consider three 'gender filters'.
* Explore situational factors on being masculine or feminine.
* Consider the virtues of 'true womanhood' and the aspirations of 'true manhood'.
* Explore the possibility of being 'something completely different'.

Role models and model roles

We often think of a role model as someone we admire or emulate. We see something in this person that we want for ourselves, whether it be the way they look, the way they behave or the talents they possess. Role models in the media are often 'model roles' to which we are supposed to aspire. Role models are sometimes living personifications of the so-called perfect gender roles. If you have ever watched a drag show or some other form of gender performance, one thing becomes clear. You have to have a sense of what constitutes a 'real woman' or a 'real man' to appreciate many of the jokes and references.

Although drag shows exaggerate the paraphernalia and performance of gender, they also leaves us with the message that true womanhood or true manhood is only something that real men and real women can perform. We like to think 'being a woman' or 'being a man' comes naturally, but often it is not as easy as it sounds. Before we consider what it takes to be a 'real woman' or a 'real man', let's look more closely at the 'nature' of gender stereotypes.

QUIZ: LIVING UP TO EXPECTATIONS: DO YOU MEASURE UP?

At the heart of the 'different planet' approach to the roles of women, men and relationships are gender-role stereotypes. As with all stereotypes, they are rigid and present a picture very much in black-and-white terms (binary). There isn't much room for ambiguity or shades of grey. Thus they appeal to the people with the pre-programmed tendency to seek simplicity.

Opposite is a list of questions to see if, in stereotypical terms, you are 'one of the girls' or 'one of the boys'. In keeping with this black-and-white view of gender roles, you only have two options for your answers.

* Your first option is **ABSOLUTELY YES**. That means an unqualified **YES**. No ifs, buts or maybes.
* Your second option is just plain **NO**. If it isn't **ABSOLUTELY YES**, then it has to be **NO**. Again, there's no in-between.

Here are the questions:

		A	**B**
1.	Are you powerful?	ABSOLUTELY YES	NO
2.	Are you strong?	ABSOLUTELY YES	NO
3.	Are you active?	ABSOLUTELY YES	NO
4.	Are you competent?	ABSOLUTELY YES	NO
5.	Are you efficient?	ABSOLUTELY YES	NO
6.	Are you goal-oriented?	ABSOLUTELY YES	NO
7.	Are you independent?	ABSOLUTELY YES	NO
8.	Are you assertive?	ABSOLUTELY YES	NO
9.	Are you competitive?	ABSOLUTELY YES	NO
10.	Are you logical?	ABSOLUTELY YES	NO
11.	Are you adventurous?	ABSOLUTELY YES	NO
12.	Are you ambitious?	ABSOLUTELY YES	NO
13.	Are you dominant?	ABSOLUTELY YES	NO
14.	Are you tough?	ABSOLUTELY YES	NO
15.	Are you decisive?	ABSOLUTELY YES	NO
16.	Are you emotional?	ABSOLUTELY YES	NO
17.	Are you relationship-oriented?	ABSOLUTELY YES	NO
18.	Are you nurturing?	ABSOLUTELY YES	NO
19.	Are you co-operative?	ABSOLUTELY YES	NO
20.	Are you intuitive?	ABSOLUTELY YES	NO
21.	Are you passive?	ABSOLUTELY YES	NO
22.	Are you submissive?	ABSOLUTELY YES	NO
23.	Are you compassionate?	ABSOLUTELY YES	NO
24.	Are you tender?	ABSOLUTELY YES	NO
25.	Are you talkative?	ABSOLUTELY YES	NO
26.	Are you gentle?	ABSOLUTELY YES	NO
27.	Are you tactful?	ABSOLUTELY YES	NO
28.	Are you sensitive?	ABSOLUTELY YES	NO
29.	Are you concerned about appearance?	ABSOLUTELY YES	NO
30.	Are you helpful?	ABSOLUTELY YES	NO
31.	Did you answer ALL 'absolutely yes' or ALL 'no' to questions 1 to 15?	ABSOLUTELY YES	NO
32.	Did you answer ALL 'absolutely yes' or ALL 'no' to questions 16 to 30?	ABSOLUTELY YES	NO

SCORING

Your scores can range from (minus) -15 to 100.

Men

* Questions 1 to 15: for each ABSOLUTELY YES, give yourself one point
* Questions 16 to 30: for each ABSOLUTELY YES, take off one point
* Bonus: Give yourself 85 points if you answered
  (a) ABSOLUTELY YES to question 31 and zero for (b) NO

Women

* Questions 16 to 30: for each ABSOLUTELY YES, give yourself one point
* Questions 1 to 15: for each ABSOLUTELY YES, take off one point
* Bonus: Give yourself 85 points if you answered
  (a) ABSOLUTELY YES to question 32 and zero for (b) NO

100 per cent real woman; 100 per cent real man

If you scored a perfect 100 you are the living personification of the gender stereotype.

A close second

If you scored between 11 and 13 points, then you come a close second. You answered a couple of answers wrong and have two choices ahead of you: first, you could work harder at becoming a 'real woman' or a 'real man' to achieve gender perfection or you could just stop trying so hard and instead be a more balanced human being. Join 'the rest of us'.

The rest of us

If you scored less than zero, then welcome to the real world. You are not a 'real man' or a 'real woman'. More likely you are 'one in a million' or 'just one of the guys'. Gender-role stereotypes set impossible ideals and striving for them can be incredibly stressful.

The fact is that most of us are in the 'the rest of us' category. There's nothing wrong with us, the problem lies with the label. If a person has to change to fit a label, it is time for a rethink.

The poem in the introduction (see page 6) unleashed a torrent of alternatives for genders, sexualities and terms that people might use to describe themselves in relation to other people. I also posed the question 'Why so many options?'. They were attempts to reflect the infinite variations in human gender and sexuality. Some may quibble that these terms are just variations on a theme; but this theme invariably centres on stereotypes and stereotypes only obscure the variations in human gender and sexuality.

The gender agenda

Let's consider some of the ways in which we acquire our gender roles. Some psychological research focuses primarily on our behaviours, it asks: 'How do we come to behave in gender-appropriate ways?'. At the most basic level, we learn behaviours and attitudes as a direct result of our social interactions. We call this social learning. The basis of this 'social learning theory' is that our actions have consequences. Therefore, we tend to repeat actions and behaviour patterns for which we are rewarded. Conversely, we tend to avoid repeating those behaviour patterns for which we are punished or not rewarded. These rewards or punishments may simply be the statements, gestures or facial expressions of others (parents, teachers, peers and so on).

Praise and criticism have a powerful effect on our behaviour. For example, boys are often actively discouraged from doing 'girl things', such as playing with dolls. Girls may be rewarded with phrases that emphasize her nurturing abilities and her fledgling motherhood role. Girls and boys quickly learn the behaviour that will gain them the most rewards and fewest punishments. This includes how they speak, how they interact with others, how they play and what clothes they wear. Even when playing with the dressing-up box, boys who choose 'girl' clothing are more likely to get a negative reaction than do girls who choose 'boy' clothes.

We also learn gender roles by imitation. This is known as 'modelling', something we briefly discussed at the beginning of this chapter. Our first role models are most often our parents or carers. Children like to explore and try out different things and they tend to model the friendly adults and those whom they see as being powerful. Most often this means the adults with access to the most rewards. We can see the vestiges of the modelling process in the body language of adults. We subconsciously mirror the body language, volume and tone of voice of those with whom we have rapport. We get on someone's 'wavelength' by synchronizing our body language.

We can also see that there are early developmental aspects to the way we learn gender roles. When children learn that gender is a constant and that they aren't going to swap over, they often begin to exaggerate their gender role. Psychologists conclude that children do this to make boundaries and expectations clearer. It is the first time we really begin to use the law of excluded middle. The boundaries between gender-appropriate toy and clothing choices (made firstly by parents and then by their children) are adhered to more rigidly. It is easy to view this developmental stage out of context and infer that children are naturally making these choices. It is true to say that gender-role conformity has more to do with the child's inner motivation at this time. External motivation in the form of rewards is a bonus. However, it is important to acknowledge the social reinforcement that preceded this stage. Rather than being a natural development it is a planned consequence of socialization.

Within various processes we can see the influence of other people, groups or organizations as 'agents of socialization'. This sounds ominous but simply means that significant people, affiliations and sources have an effect on shaping and reinforcing our gender roles. They include our parents, our teachers and our peers. The mass media may also have a strong impact on our attitudes to gender roles. Television broadcasting monitoring research consistently finds that women are under-represented in television programmes. Males are more likely to be seen giving instructions to females. Advertisements depict traditional gender roles in terms of attitudes, behaviour and personalities. When dealing with matters of sexuality, gay people are often portrayed stereotypically: as crossing gender boundaries. Gay, lesbian and bisexual characters are often portrayed as figures of fun, baddies or victims. The not-so-subtle message is that crossing gender-role boundaries has harsh consequences; people are going to laugh at you, hate you or hurt you.

Even from this brief excursion into the process of acquiring gender roles, we can see that matters are rarely, if ever, left to chance (or nature).

Domino theory and gender jeopardy

All too often we label things masculine or feminine. Why are ships and cars called 'she'? We do it with inanimate objects, personality traits and even the chemicals in the human body: hormones. This is part of the all-or-nothing approach that we explored earlier in the chapter.

Think about a behavioural trait, such as athleticism, a psychological trait, such as sociability, or even a physical characteristic, such as height. We talk about people being athletic or not athletic. However, aren't there degrees of athleticism? We talk about people being sociable or unsociable, but is it an either/or condition? We talk about people being short or tall, but where is the cut-off point for each definition? We know that we can sort people into black-and-white categories, but the question is, should we? Does the variation of human characteristics, abilities and experience all collapse into all-or-nothing, or the either/or categories?

The Living Up to Expectations quiz on page 49 conveys the idea that for gender-role stereotypes, the associated personality traits are all supposed to line up. People can only be real women or men if they stick to the appropriate side of the great gender divide. I have argued that binary categories are interconnected, that everything needs to be aligned and any crossover at any point in the chain puts the integrity of gender in jeopardy. I have talked about the ideology of gender-role stereotypes being a systematic interrelated set of beliefs from which we, in Western cultures, find it difficult to escape. Both these theories are based on the domino theory that if one falls they all fall, resulting in chaos.

Having considered the roles of men and women from a number of angles in order to tease out some of the filters we use to view gender, let's pull some of those themes together.

Gender filters

In the early 1990s, psychologist Sandra Bem put forward the idea that we view gender through three main filters (which she calls lenses): **biological essentialism**, **androcentrism** and **gender polarization**. These are just alternative phrases for some of the issues we have been talking about.

Biological essentialism describes our primary focus on reproductive biology as the principal sign of gender difference. Androcentrism simply means 'male-centred'. You may also encounter the term **phallocentric**, which means 'penis-centred'. In Western cultures, all things masculine are prized more highly than those considered feminine. Gender is based on male values and things are viewed primarily from a male perspective. Gender polarization is another way of saying 'battle of the sexes' or 'different planets'. To polarize is to divide into two groups of views: it describes the tension between binary categories.

Rather than acting independently, these three filters interact to separate men and women unequally. We have the basic biology that informs our views of social roles. Our need for simple structure means we are drawn to extremes so that clearer patterns emerge. The process of categorization invites comparison, which in turn leads to judgement as to which is superior. Such judgements come from the perspective that wields the power. Power and potency are synonymous with male sexual performance – all of which brings us back to the zeroes and ones of our respective genital shapes and the relative positions we hold in the hierarchy. There does not seem to be any opportunity for a middle course, so we exclude it. It's all-or-nothing.

We can see how these three gender filters (lenses) work together to great a coherent view of the world. The problem with lenses and filters is that they may also change or distort our perceptions, which means they aren't necessarily good for every situation.

Exercise: Situationally yours

We often talk about our personalities being relatively stable (like a leopard that can't change its spots) and as having a recognizable set of traits that make us who we are. We may describe ourselves as shy or outgoing, introvert or extrovert, sociable or unsociable and so on.

When I presented you with a list of thirty traits in the Living Up To Expectations quiz (see page 49), you were given the choice of ABSOLUTELY YES or NO. Many people find these forced-choice questions difficult to complete. So let's approach things from a different angle. Opposite are two grids, each containing a cluster of personality traits. You need to decide how much of each of these qualities you possess overall.

* Use the number range from 0 to 100.
* If you give a trait 0 it means 'not at all' and if you rate it as 100, it means 'totally', i.e. 100 per cent.
* You should use 50 as the exact mid-point, or average, and you can use any number in the range.
* You will see that there are seven columns. Put your scores in the first column.

PERSONALITY TRAITS: *CLUSTER ONE*

Trait	1	2	3	4	5	6	7
Independent							
Dominant							
Active							
Competitive							
Ambitious							
Tough							
Powerful							
Assertive							
Competent							
Strong							
Adventurous							
Efficient							
Logical							
Goal-oriented							
Decisive							
Total Score							

PERSONALITY TRAITS: *CLUSTER TWO*

Trait:	1	2	3	4	5	6	7
Intuitive							
Sensitive							
Submissive							
Compassionate							
Tender							
Helpful							
Gentle							
Tactful							
Passive							
Concerned about appearance							
Talkative							
Emotional							
Relationship-oriented							
Nurturing							
Co-operative							
Total Score							

Now do the same exercise, but responding to the following considerations:

* **Column 2:** Think about all of your personality traits in relation to the times you spend with your current partner (or your most recent partner). Alternatively, you can put yourself in their shoes and think how they might rate you.
* **Column 3:** Think about someone in your life who is accountable, younger or subordinate to you in some way. It can be a child, student, employee and so on. Rate yourself in relation to your interaction with this person. Alternatively, you can put yourself in their shoes and think about how they might rate you.
* **Column 4:** Think about someone to whom you are accountable such as your employer, team leader, headmaster, lecturer and so on. Rate yourself in relation to your interaction with this person. Alternatively, you can put yourself in their shoes and think how they might rate you.
* **Column 5:** Imagine you are ill with a cold. You have a headache, a sore throat and a runny nose. You feel miserable. Rate yourself on each of the personality traits.
* **Column 6:** Imagine you've just won the lottery or just learned of that big promotion. Rate yourself on the traits you display.
* **Column 7:** Think of yourself as a child and rate yourself on the traits you displayed.

Did your scores change or did they remain constant?

Cluster One represents some of the traits that comprise the concept of **masculinity**. Cluster Two represents the traits that comprise **femininity**.

* To find your masculinity score: take your total in column one of Cluster One and divide it by 150.
* To find your femininity score: take your total in column one of Cluster Two and divide it by 150.

MASCULINITY _____   FEMININITY _____

This is, of course, a marked improvement from ticking one of two boxes, labelled M and F. However, we can see that our scores for masculinity and femininity may vary from column to column. Rather than being separated by a hard crisp line, we can see that the boundaries are, at best, fuzzy. It's a little blurry, rather like an impressionist's painting. We have to conclude that slightly different versions of masculinity and femininity are performed by the same person at different times and in different circumstances. So which one is the real you?

Real women

Images of real women that conform to gender-role stereotypes invariably seem too good to be true. They are often based on unsustainable expectations and views of traditional femininity from some mythical golden age.

In the 1960s, the historian Barbara Welter coined the term 'the cult of womanhood' from an analysis of the new role created for upper and middle class white women during the mid-19th century. Many of her observations are still applicable to the idealized view of womanhood that persists today, which, although they are not lived up to in their extreme form in the real world still, at the very least, serve to cultivate feelings of guilt. Welter suggested that womanhood is based on the four cardinal virtues of piety, purity, submissiveness and domesticity. We might consider four female characterizations to represent these four virtues:

Earth Mother, Nice Girl, Little Sister and Domestic Goddess.

EARTH MOTHER

The Earth Mother, symbolizing piety, is the archetypal woman whose function is to care for others, particularly the weak and vulnerable, putting the needs of others before her own. She is warm, tender and caring. Whenever cases of parental cruelty to children are reported in the press, it is often the mother who receives the harshest treatment. It's as if the cruelty goes against her 'maternal instinct'. This is also seen when women leave their children.

The Earth Mother is defined in terms of what she does for others. Needless to say, a woman cast in this role, has to deny her own needs to a great extent. Real women should be 'needless and not heard'. There is an element of self-sacrifice attached to this role. Thus, what is good for those around the Earth Mother is not always good for the Earth Mother herself. Who cares for her?

This female gender-role stereotype incorporates traits such as compassion, tenderness and nurturing.

NICE GIRL

The Nice Girl (good girl) symbolizes purity. She is the eternal daddy's girl, the true woman who is always a little girl at heart. These women are neat and tidy and look after their appearance. Nice Girls look after their bodies and watch what they eat. In keeping with the double standard, true womanhood means 'knees together' not 'legs akimbo'. The opposite of a 'red-blooded male' is the 'bad girl'. A woman who transgresses the illusory boundary between 'good girls' and 'bad girls', is (at least) likely to be subjected to various terms of abuse, such as slut, slag, whore or 'loose woman'.

LITTLE SISTER

The figure of Little Sister represents submissiveness. However, we may represent this today as being passive and non-confrontational. There isn't supposed to be any sibling rivalry between the sister and her brother. Worldly Big Brother knows best. Homely Little Sister is supposed to know her place. Instead of confrontation, the Little Sister (little princess) is supposed to 'wrap Big Brother round her little finger' to get what she wants. Furthermore, the Big Brother isn't supposed to know that the Little Sister got her own way.

DOMESTIC GODDESS

Two partners may go out to work and be in paid employment, but the domestic responsibilities are still more likely to rest with the woman in a male–female partnership. Domesticity and femininity are linked. Hints on being a good wife from 1950s magazines now seem laughable by today's standards. Nevertheless, the implications of these guidelines still have an impact today. Although it may not be necessary for a woman to put a ribbon in her hair before her husband arrives home, the expectation is for females to maintain domestic standards. And of course, she should never be too tired to fulfil her conjugal duties.

According to the 'cult of womanhood', it is this combination of roles that brings happiness and 'power' to women's lives. In the context of appropriate gender roles, power equates to protection and freedom from persecution. This, in turn, brings a limited kind of happiness or, rather, relief from unhappiness. However, we should not overlook the great changes in women's roles during the 20th century. Nevertheless, the four pillars of the cult of womanhood are clearly present in the 'different planet' approach to gender and relationships.

Today, in the real world, women's roles are not necessarily defined in terms of the significant men in their lives (although there is still a glass ceiling in terms of women's status in society at large). Nevertheless, we can still see that women's roles have incorporated many of the characteristics and aspirations associated with traditional female roles, albeit more subtly. All of the four virtues are co-operative and relationship-oriented.

We will discuss the implications of this later in the chapter. Meanwhile, let's take a look at what it means to be a 'real man'.

Real men

The male gender role has been less amenable to change over the years. In comparison with women's roles, there have been relatively few changes in the expectations of men. In many ways masculinity is still about being Number One. The components of 'true manhood' are essentially anti-femininity, independence, superiority, status, power and toughness. However, one of the most important aspects of male identity is that men are defined in terms of what they are not. It's a kind of manhood by default; 'real men' are simply 'not women'. This of course sounds too obvious to even mention, but a defining feature of masculinity is that it over-labours the point.

In the 1970s, the psychologist and gender theorist Richard Brannon encapsulated the essential components of manhood in four cardinal aspirations, which I have updated and amended for this book. They are:

Tough Guy, Big Shot, Hell Raiser and No Girly Stuff.

TOUGH GUY

Enter the Hollywood tough guy, the all-action super hero. It's Captain Sturdy Oak. The Sturdy Oak was Brannon's original term. An oak tree is very much a symbol of strength, independence and self-reliance (and also tradition). It is good to have someone to rely on, as long as that person isn't just 'putting on a brave face'. 'Big boys don't cry' is a phrase often repeated over and over to little boys. They eventually get the message: emotion is something to be controlled or suppressed – it's something that girls do.

BIG SHOT

'Real men' are successful, gain status and respect and have the need to have power over others. Male gender-role stereotypes include traits like ambition, competition and dominance. Unfortunately, this attitude also spills over in other relationships, with women and other men. It's all about being a winner, being Number One, being someone in the eyes of others.

HELL RAISER

The Hell Raiser never lets anyone get the better of him. Hell Raisers just like to give people hell, sometimes for hell's sake. Aggression and violence are legitimate means to an end and that end justifies the means. Of course, associated with this aspiration is hard and fast living and risk taking. The Hell Raiser encapsulates aspects of the male gender-role stereotype, such as adventurousness, toughness and activeness.

NO GIRLY STUFF

This is manhood or masculinity by default. It is defined in terms of what it is not, not by what it is. To be a real man, you have to be different from a woman. This means avoiding the girly (sissy) stuff or anything that might be considered feminine. Real men expunge any trace of sensitivity, tenderness, gentleness and emotion. Young boys quickly learn that it's not good to be labelled a sissy. By contrast, 'tomboy' behaviour in girls is often viewed as endearing, although only up until adolescence.

Ironically, for straight men, spending too much time with your girlfriend might be considered 'girly stuff', especially when you could be out carousing with the boys. It's interesting that gay and lesbian relationships can also be affected by the 'no girly stuff' rule. This is especially the case when a relationship very much follows the traditional male/female pattern. Among some gay men, it is considered desirable to be thought of as 'straight-acting' as opposed to 'camp'.

Common to all of these components of true manhood is a sense of self-evaluation in terms of an external benchmark. Three of the aspirations are goal-orientation, power and strength and one is about negating weakness.

It is important to recognize that this also involves suppressing or denying any sense of an internal or personal standard. The male gender role boasts independence but screams compliance. How can a man achieve his own personal best if his internal standards or his opinion don't even enter into it? Much of the male role is predicated on bluster and bravado, what the psychotherapist George Weinberg calls the 'masculine pretence'. You may be a real man, but are you authentic? Are you true to yourself?

Exercise: The Real You?

Before we consider 'something completely different', I'd like you to pause briefly and consider the times in your life that you were not true to you self.

If you are a woman, was there ever a time when you felt compelled to be an earth mother, a nice girl, the little sister or the domestic goddess; or if you are a man, was there ever a time when you felt compelled to be a tough guy, a big shot, a hell-raiser or avoided the girly stuff? If so, make a brief note of some examples:

How did you feel at the time?

Does it still happen to you?

Do you think any of us have a choice or is that just the way things are?

Ask someone significant in your life if they find that these pressures also apply to them.

Do you know anyone who seems to have escaped these pressures? If so, ask them how they managed it.

Something completely different

We have begun to emerge from the shadows of the monolithic ideals of real men and real women. In everyday conversations we use a variety of terms for gender roles. We talk about girl power and about lads and ladettes. We talk about geezer birds, women who are just one of the lads. We talk about new men who embody many of the characteristics traditionally associated with women. We talk about himbos and bimbos, which are caricatures of masculinity and femininity. We routinely use the word 'guys' to refer to either gender. Rather than gender-defending we are, in many ways, gender-blending (Kate Bornstein's phrases). Our use of language at least suggests that we accept the concept of multiple masculinities and multiple femininities existing side-by-side.

In the 1970s, instead of viewing masculinity and femininity at the opposite ends of the same continuum, Sandra Bem argued that they should be measured separately. This is why you calculated one score for each. She proposed four possible combinations. The Situationally Yours exercise on page 55 provides an approximation to her scheme, so let's look at how these combinations apply to you. We need to apply that all-pervasive binary thinking again and create two categories for each score:

    0 to 50   = LOW
    50 to 100 = HIGH

Now apply these high/low categories to the following table:

	LOW MASCULINITY	HIGH MASCULINITY
LOW FEMININITY	UNDIFFERENTIATED	MASCULINE
HIGH FEMININITY	FEMININE	ANDROGYNOUS

We arrive at four basic gender patterns. We have been discussing the concepts of masculine and feminine throughout the book; the new term 'undifferentiated' means 'nothing much to go on'; and androgyny represents someone who has a balance of traits associated with masculinity and femininity. Androgyny has often been used to describe people who seem midway between two extremes, but this is incorrect. Androgyny more accurately describes someone who is both highly masculine and highly feminine. Although at first this may seem difficult to grasp, what this means is a psychologically rounded human being.

Sex, Lies and Stereotypes

There is nothing intrinsically masculine or feminine about personal traits and emotions, only the labels we apply to separate them. More accurately they are all human traits. However, it was discovered that the masculinity score was the better predictor of psychological well-being. Thus, to a degree, the test had (unwittingly) incorporated the biases of traditional gender stereotypes. There was a higher degree of self-determination described by masculine characteristics while, by contrast, the feminine traits incorporated child-like qualities and self-sacrifice. We can see how these reflect the cardinal pillars of true womanhood (see pages 57–59) and true manhood (see pages 59–61). Nevertheless, Bem's work still represented a significant leap in awareness of gender issues – getting us to see masculinity and femininity as separate entities rather than as one entity being expressed at the expense of the other.

The concepts of new men and new women can be viewed as attempts to balance our gender roles. However, whenever we talk about a man 'getting in touch with his feminine' side we are unwittingly perpetuating the myth that personality traits and emotions know how to 'talk sides'; emotions have no consciousness, rather it is merely the way we choose to conceptualize them. Do children need two gender-stereotyped parents? Maybe one psychologically rounded parent would be better. There is also the danger that if women want to succeed in a 'man's world', then they need to adopt more male traits. To be a more rounded human being this may be true, but not at the expense of other traits considered 'female'. If we continue to overvalue masculinity and undervalue femininity we merely end up undermining humanity.

In many ways we have begun to exercise more control over our lives. With the proliferation of communication and information technology, our world-view is no longer controlled by those who control the written word. In Western cultures we are able to mix-and-match our information sources. We have access to billions of pages of information on the Internet. In some ways, such choice means that we have the knowledge to become our own immaculate conceptions. Such knowledge gives us the power to play with gender. We're ripe for a rethink.

Conclusion: Different planets and black holes

When we were very young we knew what it meant to be a boy or girl. Through play, consciously and unconsciously, we tested the boundaries and limits. When we were six or seven we came to realize that our gender was a constant. Girls would become women as sure as boys would become men. The playground of gender became a more serious affair. Boys and girls took up opposite sides and we played our gender roles 'for all we were worth'. Nothing prevented us from playing in the middle of the playground, nevertheless we didn't. Many years later we discovered that our gender roles are indeed the measure of our worth and we still play hard to make the grade.

We talk about schooldays being the best days of our lives, albeit through rose-tinted lenses. Remember when we used to sit cross-legged in front of the teacher at story time eagerly awaiting the next instalment? Many of those stories were allegories and metaphors endlessly retold not only to entertain but to shape the way we viewed the world. However, although we aren't those little children any more (except maybe at heart), we still enjoy a good story, and we still use the language of the playground to talk about gender, relationships and sex.

The exaggerated roles we acted out as children were the first real steps in our attachment to gender stereotypes. It was the moment when we were typeset ready for the gender printing press. We now reproduce endlessly the patterns of expectation. However, gender stereotypes operate at the level of 'one-label-fits-all', and I can't resist telling you a little story to emphasize the point.

Procrustes was the ancient Greek forerunner of Basil Fawlty. He was a wicked giant who welcomed strangers and offered them a bed for the night. It wasn't a bed, breakfast and evening meal arrangement, more a 'one-size-fits-all' kind of place. He only had one guest bed, and if guests were too long for the bed, he chopped off their legs. If they were too short, he lengthened them on a rack.

There is a strong parallel with gender-role stereotypes. We are often expected to distort our behaviour and experience with more than just a little metaphorical chopping and stretching. It's a case of male and female 'gender mutilation'. Often it seems as though we actually get more choice in booking a bed for the night than we do about our gender roles.

Our gender roles are genital metaphors. They are animated scripts based on the shapes of our genitals. Can we really do justice to the variety of human expression and experience by always bringing the focus back to the penis or the vagina? We often think of the labels of 'male' and 'female' as descriptions, but they are really wishful thinking. It is based on the wish to make the world a simpler more predictable place. However, we

Sex, Lies and Stereotypes

have to return to the fundamental question of whether two labels are enough. What about the variety in the middle ground we exclude from this binary view?

We have seen in this chapter how we change according to the demands of a situation. We also acknowledge that different versions of masculinity and femininity can co-exist in our culture from the language we use. Surely labels should be about description not prescription. People shouldn't have to change to fit the labels. Maybe we even need to question whether we need labels at all. Shouldn't we all aspire to become more rounded human beings?

In this section we exposed some of the black holes in the 'different planet' approach to gender roles and human relationships. In the next section we need to go back to basics and fundamentally challenge the assumptions on which the 'different planet' approach is based. At the heart of it, our anatomy is supposedly our destiny, so that's where we will start.

PART TWO

Back to Basics

4

Gender Blueprints:
Is Anatomy Our Destiny?

We live dissected into isolated communities and individuals; in our bodily sensitivity, we are one species – Don Hanlon Johnson, modern-day philosopher

The sense of an inside is no less important for men's sexual subjectivity than for women's – Jessica Benjamin, modern-day feminist theorist and psychoanalyst

For now we see through a glass darkly; but then face to face: now I know in part; but then shall I know even as I am known – 1 Corinthians 13:12; Bible (King James Version, 1611)

PREVIEW

In this chapter we will:

* Consider some of the facts and fictions about human anatomy in the form of a brief quiz.
* Reconsider the biological symbols of female and male as metaphors for human development.
* Offer a 'back to basics' review of human physiology and anatomy.
* Critically review the 'Egg and Sperm Race' and how our biology is viewed through the lenses of gender stereotypes.

A question of difference?

In a somewhat facetious description of the differences between male and female genitals, Eric Berne, the founder of transactional analysis, describes the genitals of the male as 'an aggressive delivery system' and those of the female as being 'equipped to encourage and handle... deliveries'. Joking aside, there is a serious point to be made here. Isn't this how we see male and female genitals? The male genitals are seen as the active agent and the female genitals are seen as being the passive recipient. It's as if the sole purpose of the female genitals is to patiently wait to be 'completed' by the insertion of the penis. The description is really all about sex for procreation and not sex for recreation.

So what? Isn't all this just making a big deal out of a throw-away quip? The short answer is no and the long answer involves going back to our biological roots to see if this wisecrack stands up to scrutiny. We like to think that biology is an objective science with no room for interpretation of the facts, but that simply is not true. As with any aspect of being human, our perceptions do shape our reality. So firstly, let's have a look at the short quiz on human anatomy opposite to help tease out some of the issues we will explore in this chapter.

Blueprints of difference

The genitals are used to describe the difference between men and women. So, let's begin by looking at those differences, starting with the biological symbols for the female and the male. The biological symbol for the female comes from a depiction of the hand mirror of the Roman goddess of love and fertility, Venus, who is also the goddess of springtime and flowers. This is also the symbol for the planet Venus. For the male, the biological symbol is a representation of the spear and shield of the Roman god of war and aggression, Mars, who was also, at one point, the god of agriculture.

Male   Female

Sex, Lies and Stereotypes

HUMAN ANATOMY QUIZ

1. Women are the biologically weaker sex. **True or false?** _____
2. Men have male hormones, and women have female hormones. **True or false?** _____
3. Women have testosterone. **True or false?** _____
4. The anus has an erotic capacity for both men and women. **True or false?** _____
5. The anus has an erotic capacity irrespective of sexual orientation. **True or false?** _____
6. The correct name for the female genitals is the vagina. **True or false?** _____
7. A clitoris is a like a tiny penis. **True or false?** _____
8. The clitoris is the only organ in the human body with the sole function of sexual pleasure. **True or false?** _____
9. The ovaries and the testes are formed from the same embryonic tissue. **True or false?** _____
10. Biologically the 'default' value of humans is female. **True or false?** _____
11. Women are incomplete men? **True or false?** _____
12. Men and women are so different that they may as well be from different planets. **True or false?** _____

The answers are discussed throughout the chapter and summarized on page 84.

There is really nothing about human biology that can be associated with these symbols (and the respective planets) apart from the stereotypical roles of women and men; although one might conclude that the spear of Mars could symbolize a penis. However, I'd like to use these familiar symbols as a device to explain biological developmental processes and to propose a model of human similarity.

I have been emphasizing the effects of perceptual filters on our view of the world and these two symbols illustrate this perfectly. On the face of it, the symbols look very different until we realize that a great deal of the difference simply relates to the angle at which we view them. The differences would be less pronounced if we switched them round. The question is, which one should move? This seems an unnecessary question, but I want to bring in a rationale for how we view gender, because we all see the world from a particular angle.

Gender theorist and performance artist, Kate Bornstein argues that the perfect gender is male and that it is the standard by which we judge all else. In one of a series of quizzes on gender identity, Bornstein asks: 'Were you born with and do you still have a penis?'. In the quest for 'perfect gender', the person who answers 'yes' to this question is immediately conferred the enormous advantage of 250 points. Wrapped up in Bornstein's light-hearted approach is the significance that it is indeed still a man's world, socially, politically and economically.

Having a penis confers an (arbitrary) advantage, which is why I placed the Mars–male symbol first. Being male means that a person is more likely to rise higher up life's ladder. From the moment a child is born, it is assigned its gender on the basis of the presence or absence of a penis. If a penis is clearly visible it's a boy, if not it's a girl. This gender assignment is based on the primacy of the male organ.

In the Introduction I mentioned Adam and Eve and the Garden of Eden. As Adam was created first, this creates the impression that the default value of the human race is male and that females were an afterthought, the side-kick and subordinate player to the male's starring role. Now, consider the baby girls who are abandoned all around the world because their parents wanted boys. Why? Well, in some societies males are more highly valued than females. We also talk about women being the fairer, but also the weaker sex. Such assertions must not go unchallenged.

We need to discover whether it is maleness or femaleness that is the default value of the human race. Although there are exceptions, we have two basic variations for the human species. I'm fully aware that there are people who, for whatever reason, don't fit this narrow scheme. However, for the purposes of advancing the argument, I want to work with the black-and-white (binary) view. The question we are really asking is, 'Are women really incomplete men or are men really women with a bit added on?'. I have asked this many times and often get looks of incredulity; maybe you feel the same way. However, to make some sense of this seemingly senseless question we need to discuss briefly our chromosomes.

X and why?

In simple terms, genes are the units of heredity, such as eye-colour and facial shape, passed down from parents to their offspring. Chromosomes are long, stringy coiled packets of genes that carry this heredity information and human genes are encoded on 23 pairs of chromosomes (46 in all). For females, all chromosomes are X-shaped. However for males, one of the pair is Y-shaped (because one branch of the X appears to be missing). It is this difference in the last pair of chromosomes that determines the genetic sex of an embryo. For a female the 23rd chromosome is XX, and for a male it is XY. The first item in the pair (X) comes from the egg of the mother. The father's sperm produces the difference in the second chromosome. So, an X sperm produces XX (girl), and a Y sperm produces XY (boy). The Y chromosome is also missing some of the genes of the X chromosome, which means it doesn't protect the male so well from hereditary diseases. For a female, an abnormal gene from both parents is required to cause disease; it needs to affect both of the X chromosomes. For the male, there is only one X to affect. Biologically then, males are the weaker sex. No question.

In *Zeros and Ones*, Sadie Plant goes so far as to say that the prototypes we have for human beings are mainly double-female (XX) or half-female/half-male (XY). So, effectively, what we have is the 'egg' as the default and the sperm producing the variation. Although there are many variations on these two basic prototypes (with additional X and Y chromosomes), it is not possible to have a double male (YY). For instance, it is possible to have many variations on the theme of XY (up to four people per thousand are born with one of these variations). The most common alternative pattern includes additional X chromosomes (XXY), which results in a male birth, although the development of male genitals is hindered. Occasionally, there can be even more extra chromosomes with XXXY and XXXXY patterns and, occasionally, so-called 'super-females' are born with extra X chromosomes, such as XXX. There have even been cases of XXXX and XXXXX patterns. With so-called 'super-males', an extra Y chromosome is present (XYY). It is even possible to have a single X (actually Xo), but never a single Y. The X from the egg always forms the basic platform. This, I contend, gives us enough evidence to conclude that we should look at gender from the female perspective.

Let's take our two biological symbols and put the female symbol first and look at maleness from a slightly different angle:

Female   Male reviewed

It's amazing that with a simple switch of perspective the two symbols look very similar. In fact, the similarities outweigh the differences. Both have a large circle and a long (vertical) line. The only difference is the crossbar for the female and the head of the arrow for the male. Okay, it's a neat little rhetorical manoeuvre and it seems to make intuitive sense, however, is there any more scientific evidence, other than genes and chromosomes, for looking at things from a female perspective?

You may accept that we have 22 (and a half) pairs of chromosomes in common, but surely these relatively small differences become more pronounced as development proceeds. After all, a penis is a penis and a vagina is a vagina. There's no denying that they look very different, no matter what angle you view them from. But just how significant is this physical difference?

VENUS OR PENIS?

Once the egg is fertilized it begins to divide to produce more cells. First, a hollow ball of cells develops, then this begins to fold and differentiate to form an embryo. Now, regardless of the chromosome carried by the sperm, there isn't really any anatomical difference until about the sixth week in the womb. Up until this point, the genitals of the embryo are a kind of indistinct collection of structures, a vague arrangement of bumps and grooves. They may be different at the chromosomal level, but they both have the capacity to go down the female route or the male route as both contain reproductive structures capable of developing a female reproductive system and a male reproductive system. It is only in the seventh or eighth week of development that some kind of distinction occurs and, even then, the difference is minute.

However, at around three months things really begin to change. With an XY (male) embryo, two hormones are produced: one stimulates the structure of the male reproductive system, while the other inhibits the structure of the female reproductive system and makes it degenerate. By contrast, for the XX (female) embryo, there is little hormone production, but the female reproductive system develops nevertheless. The embryo may be XY (boy), but if the 'squirts' of hormones fail to trigger changes at the right time and in the right amounts, the embryo will automatically develop along the female route. That is to say, biology will produce a female unless given instructions to the contrary. Hence, maleness appears to be something of a detour, an exception to the rule, whereas female development is a straight line – the shortest distance between two points.

Sex, Lies and Stereotypes

Again, this process emphasizes that femaleness is the default state of the human race. From three months onwards, depending on whether the baby is going to be a girl or a boy, bits of tissue take different routes. Let's take a look at their eventual destinations.

COMPARISON OF FEMALE AND MALE GENITALIA	
Female	Male
ovaries	testes
labia majora (outer lips)	scrotum
labia minora (inner lips)	underside of penis
glans (head) of the clitoris	glans (head) of penis
shaft (erectile tissue) of clitoris	corpus cavernosum (erectile tissue)
vagina	*no comparable structure*

When located side by side in the table, structures are formed from the same embryonic tissue. So, for instance, a penis and a clitoris are formed from the same embryonic tissue; similarly, ovaries and testes are formed from the same tissue; the scrotum is formed from the same tissue as the labia majora (the outer lips); and so on. However, the notable difference is that males do not have any kind of structure that resembles a vagina, except for a feint trace where the scrotal swellings fused together. Apart from that, men and women have pretty much everything else in common. And wouldn't you know it, the only thing that men and women don't have in common is the thing we focus on most.

The collective term for female genitalia is the vulva, although we regularly we call it the 'vagina', which is actually the birth canal. So you see that when describing female genitalia in everyday language we put the emphasis on reproduction and take the emphasis off sexual pleasure. If we focus on pleasure we find that the main centres for sexual pleasure (the penis and the clitoris) in biological terms have a common origin.

Nevertheless, we focus on the superficial differences when assigning gender at birth. The presence of the penis is the primary determinant. Thus, we afford the penis a privileged position in our gender economy. Even if we do acknowledge the clitoris, we describe it as a miniature penis. If the default value of the human race is female, wouldn't it be more accurate to describe the penis as an enlarged clitoris?

Furthermore, women have separate centres for sexual gratification (the clitoris) and reproduction (the vagina), although they are wired up together. Women also have a separate structure for urination. By contrast, men have a multi-function organ (the penis) to void urine, ejaculate semen and to provide sexual pleasure. So, whereas a penis is like a 'ghetto-blaster' or 'boogie box' (with combined radio, CD and tape player), the genitals of a woman are more like 'hi-fi separates'. However, you will rarely (if ever) see this analogy appearing in biology books or being taught in schools.

As we have seen, our hormones are cited as the agents of difference in genital human development, so let's take a closer look at these.

Hormonal or nothing?

We often hear talk of hormones and their effects on human behaviour. Put simply, hormones are chemicals that circulate in the bloodstream and are produced by glands in the body. They control the actions of certain cells and organs. In everyday conversation we cite hormones as the key factors in explaining the perceived differences in female and male behaviour. This talk of male and female hormones leads us to the erroneous conclusion that men and women have different sets of chemicals. Again we see how language shapes perception while the scientific reality is slightly different.

Rather than having two totally different sets of chemicals, both males and females actually share the same hormones. We don't have an accurate figure for just how many hormones there are in the human body (it could run into the hundreds), however, we focus on a handful of hormones that we call sex hormones. Compounding this is the (often incorrect) assumption that the sex hormones are only implicated in sexual (or gender specific) behaviour.

The so-called sex hormones are androgens, most notably testosterone – which we usually call the male hormone – oestrogens (there are three) and progesterone – which we usually call the female hormones. In terms of hormone production, the differences do not relate to the kind of hormones but their relative levels; it is not an issue of quality but quantity. For instance, testosterone is produced in the testes, the ovaries and the adrenal glands; it has a regulatory function on the sex drives of both men and women, but also on fat distribution and muscle bulk. Admittedly, the average amount will differ between males and females, but both genders have it. Progesterone also helps to build and maintain bone mass and is vital to both women and men.

In *The Apartheid of Sex* Martine Rothblatt argues that, as with most aspects of being human, what we find is that rather than a fixed line between the sexes, the categories of male and female are in reality general approximations. Although it is correct to say that the majority of women cluster at one end and the majority of men cluster at the other end, there is a degree of overlap.

So, in the category of women there is some variation in biochemical levels and the same is true for the category of men. When we speak about sex differences, even on a biological level, we are really talking about the relative amounts produced. Indeed, we may find that some genetic females have more androgens than do some genetic males, at least some of the time. Men vary from each other in terms of their relative proportion of hormones, as do women.

We often focus on the differences between the sexes and overestimate them, which leads to an underestimation of the differences between people of the same sex, which are often more notable. This is yet another example of how we apply the law of excluded middle.

When we speak of difference, we inevitably make comparisons and judgements of 'superiority'. We find that maleness is often credited with a primacy and, therefore, privilege that is not supported by biological evidence. Yet, according to Kate Bornstein, men are (well-) endowed with a 250-point advantage no matter what. So, is Venus forever destined to covet Mars's powerful spear? That's the mythology. However, as we have begun to see things from the other side of Venus's looking glass (albeit darkly), maybe we should consider the envies of Mars.

Venus envy?

It has passed down into common lore (from Sigmund Freud) that women suffer from 'penis envy'. However, it is not necessarily the physical penis that is the source of envy but the social, economic and political advantage conferred on a person who possesses one. Whatever you may think of this argument, it is important to note that, for the greater part, penis-envy does not stem from women at all, but from male locker rooms. Penis enlargement operations are mainly about increasing the size of the penis in its flaccid state. We have already noted that women have a specialized structure purely for sexual arousal, so what's to envy in the penis?

The most notable difference in genital arrangements is the absence of any genital structure in men that directly corresponds to a vagina. As men seem to be the envious ones, could this envy extend to their lack of a vagina, too? Maybe men have Venus envy?

Perhaps the phenomenon of anal foreign body insertion is a clue. Medical reports provide an answer and the most striking finding of the reports in medical journals is the staggering array of objects used for male anal penetration. They include more predictable items, such as sex-toys and penis-shaped fruit and vegetables, but also potatoes and hard-boiled eggs; glass bottles, tool handles and light-bulbs have also been reported. Research reveals that male anal penetration is primarily an auto-erotic act. In fact, men are more than 28 times more likely to engage in this act than women. In addition, the majority of research reports no history of a 'gay lifestyle'. So, essentially this act is mainly carried out by heterosexual men when they are alone.

This evidence is only based on those people who sought medical attention – how many more men skilled, or lucky, in extracting the objects do not show up in the figures? And, of course, when presenting themselves for medical attention, these men do not freely admit to voluntarily inserting the objects; they may claim it was an accident or done to alleviate itching or haemorrhoids. On occasion they feign total ignorance and exclaim, 'How did that get there?'. Clearly, this is an example of the 'no girly stuff' filter kicking in.

The different planet approach advocates that a man's longing for sex concerns a spiritual search for wholeness. Evidence from anal foreign body insertion suggests that, for some men, the need to experience the 'sense of an inside' is irresistible. Generally, the anus is perceived as having an erotic capacity for only a minority of adults, most notably for gay men. However, the evidence presented here suggests that it may have a wider appeal. So let's go back to basics and review the biological evidence.

Every body needs good neighbours

Genitals and anuses are neighbours, such good neighbours in fact that we might say they are good friends. They share everything. No en-suite accommodation for these two pals, they share the same facilities. Inevitably, for most people, these comments will evoke some kind of reaction. The anus is one topic on which it is difficult to be neutral. It has become a symbol of dirtiness. So, not surprisingly, some people may think that anything concerned with anal stimulation is a wilful perversion of the natural sexual urge. However, for many people (male and female, straight and gay) the anus ia source of sexual pleasure. Anal eroticism transcends social boundaries. Let's consider the biology for a moment.

Usually out of sight, hidden by the buttocks, the anus is an external opening formed by folds of soft tissue, which give it a puckered appearance. It is richly supplied with nerve endings. Usually closed, two ring-like muscles called the (external and internal) sphincters control its opening. When used in the singular, sphincter refers to the external muscle. The anus leads into a short anal canal, a tube-like passageway, of about one inch (2.5cm) in length; this, in turn, leads into the larger rectum. The rectum is the passage through which faeces, stored further up in the colon, are excreted.

Pleasurable sensations associated with defecation are, according to the neurologist and psychotherapist Sigmund Freud, a natural part of human development. These sensations begin around the time of toilet training and are carried into adulthood, although they might not retain an overtly erotic association. The anus and the surrounding area contain tactile (touch) sensors, sensory fibres and a number of muscles that are shared directly with the genitals.

The same interactive relationship also exists between the nervous structure of the anus and genitals, so much so that it is impossible to distinguish the origin of some nerve impulses. In both men and women, irrespective of sexual orientation, when we orgasm we experience involuntary contractions (squeezing) of the sphincters. Not surprisingly then, if we voluntarily squeeze the anal sphincter, this leads to a series of muscular reactions that pull on the penis or clitoris and which may heighten sexual sensations.

It is because of this extensive interaction, that stimulation of either the genitals or the anus may produce a reaction in the other. Stimulation of the rectum can also cause stimulation of other organs by direct pressure. The front wall of the rectum is adjacent to the prostate gland and seminal vesicles in males and the rear wall of the vagina and uterus in females. It is physically possible for both men and women to experience orgasm solely from anal penetration.

The sensitivity to anal penetration and stimulation of the rectum is the same irrespective of gender or sexuality. For people for whom anal stimulation has no erotic significance, a high degree of sensitivity still exists. This all seems to confirm that, certainly in terms of the erotic capacity of the anus, we are all one species. It could be argued that a particular psychological disposition is needed to interpret anal sensations as erotic; however, given the intimate interaction between the anus and genitals, it would seem that it takes a particular kind of psychological disposition not to.

The main theme to emerge from this brief review of the anatomy of anal eroticism is that it represents another area of equivalence for men and women.

A bit of a detour

This brief review of human biology leads to the conclusion that women and men have many more similarities than differences. Our preference for black-and-white thinking distorts the perceptual filters with which we view women and men.

The biological symbols for female (Venus) and for male (Mars) are perfect to explain the whole process of sex and gender. Stripping away the similarities in the symbols leaves us with the symbols of the true male and female differences:

▬   ∨

The real difference between female and male

This remnant accurately describes the true extent of sex and gender differences. It also describes the process of embryonic development. The remaining piece of the female symbol is effectively a straight line which is the shortest distant between two points. This describes the development of the embryo along the female route. The remaining piece of the male symbol is not the shortest distance between two points, it represents a bit of a detour. This describes the development of the embryo along the male route.

Although the 'journey' is slightly different and although we may look slightly different, the end result is the same: we are both more human above all else.

Sex, Lies and Stereotypes

Life through a gender-coloured lens

Although considered an objective science, biology is not immune to interpretation through perceptual filters. I refer, of course, to the three gender filters (lenses) discussed in the last chapter: biological essentialism emphasizes the respective shapes of our genitals; androcentrism emphasizes the male perspective; and gender polarization (which applies the law of excluded middle) emphasizes the 'battle of the sexes'. Here are some examples to illustrate the use of these filters.

The first example comes from my own research that looks at gender differences in attitudes to anal and oral sex acts. Despite the biological evidence that the anus has an equivalent erotic capacity for men and women, there were gender differences in attitudes to its sexual use. The ratings for all of the participants showed that the female anus was rated more 'sexual', 'attractive' and 'positive' in comparison to the male anus. A gender breakdown in attitudes revealed the origin of this difference: female ratings mirrored the biological evidence and there was little or no difference in their ratings of male and female anuses. Put simply, the females made an objective assessment. The males, however, seem to be far more subjective in their attitudes. They tended to overestimate the sexual capacity of the female anus and underestimate the sexual capacity of the male anus. Essentially, males were over-emphasizing the permeability of the female body. Arguably, the female anus was viewed as a surrogate vagina (any hole's a goal), indicating that the gender lenses of biological essentialism drove the males' responses.

The research also looked at the opposite end of the body and looked at attitudes towards the mouth and oral sex. The results followed the same pattern. There is no biological difference between a man's and woman's mouth in terms of erotic capacity and female ratings mirror this, but, as before, males saw women's bodies as being more permeable than men's bodies. The research moved to consider sexual acts and participants were presented with four scenarios:

1. Male penis penetrating female anus (standard heterosexual).
2. Female with penis shaped object penetrating male anus (reversed heterosexual).
3. Male penis penetrating male anus (gay).
4. Female with penis shaped object penetrating female anus (lesbian).

Participants were asked to indicate which partner would have been most likely to initiate the sexual act. In the standard heterosexual couple, the male was indicated as the most likely initiator. A similar pattern was found for the gay couple, with the penetrator indicated as the more likely to initiate the sex act. These findings support the view that 'activeness' is associated with the penetrator role, whereas 'passivity' is associated with the receptive (penetrated) role. In the reversed heterosexual scenario, the male was indicated as the most likely to initiate the act. Thus the real penis took precedence over the substitute one. Attitudes were expressed in line with gender-role stereotypes, so the filters of biological essentialism and androcentrism were seen at work.

The second example comes from an academic article by pioneering biologist Emily Martin entitled *The Egg and the Sperm: How Science Has Constructed a Romance Based on Stereotypical Male-Female Roles* (1991). We could call it the Egg and Sperm Race. It reveals how traditional academic accounts of the sperm and the egg borrow heavily from gender stereotypes in explaining biological processes. Supposedly objective scientific accounts give the impression that female biological processes – and indeed women – are altogether less worthy than their male counterparts. For instance, one account focuses on the so-called wastefulness of egg production in females. Some accounts have questioned why so many eggs are formed only to die in the ovaries? However, the massive over-production of sperm is not addressed. Whereas a male is described as producing sperm, the female is described as shedding an egg. Thus, production for the male is juxtaposed with disposal for the female. Furthermore, the egg is described in stereotypically feminine terms whereas the sperm is described in stereotypically masculine terms. The egg is passively transported, it is swept along or it drifts. By contrast, the streamlined sperm actively delivers genes to the egg. They are described in terms of strength, speed and efficiency. Maybe these images mirror your own images of biological processes. Martin argues that the reality is markedly different.

The stereotypical view of sperm as a forceful penetrator was challenged in the mid-1980s when biologists discovered that a sperm's forward thrust is relatively weak. In fact, the strongest tendency shown by sperm was to pry itself off the egg rather than penetrating it. However, this caused only a minor modification to the prevailing view. Sperm were still described as attacking and penetrating, only a little less forcefully. Its role still conformed to the traditional male gender-role stereotype. It was not until the late 1980s that the egg was credited with a more active role in the process. Nevertheless, it was still very much in the context of gender stereotypes. The role of the egg was recast as an aggressive sperm-catcher, because of the inadequacy of the sperm thrust. This revision resonates with accounts of dangerous female sexuality or sirens luring hapless sailors to their doom. Even though the research strongly suggested that the egg and sperm were really mutual partners, the model of domination and submission still prevailed.

It is also at this stage in the accounts that the sperm seems to acquire a harpoon that is fired into the egg. This theme is picked up in the Sineplian/Anigavlian mythology, where the Sineplians launch their invasion of Anigavlia. The concept of the harpoon suggests speed and aggression. However, the process is more accurately described in terms of bridge building, slowly, molecule by molecule. The egg and the sperm are mutually active and interactive partners, bridging the gap together. However, we still think of the sperm as the instigator and the conqueror in keeping with the male gender-role stereotype.

So even the most basic of biological processes are distorted by the three gender filters discussed in the last chapter. We can also see how the view of bodily parts changes depending on the gender of the body. It seems difficult for us to escape the influence of gender stereotypes. After all, let's not let the biological facts get in the way of a good 'love' story.

Conclusion: Through a glass darkly

We often talk about biology as if it has a consciousness and a sense of maleness or femaleness. But biologically we are the same species, and the similarities between men and woman far outweigh the differences. Furthermore, the differences are more often quantitative and not qualitative. While our genitals may be the outward signs of our biological sex, we share a common origin and continue to share many of the same capacities and experiences.

By far the largest difference between men and women is the view we gain from gazing through different filters. However, as we have seen from the material in this chapter, there is real evidence that challenges the traditional filter of biological essentialism: we are not essentially different. There is also evidence that challenges the filter of androcentrism: biologically, maleness is not privileged.

Considering the categories of female and male, the differences within the categories are often greater than the differences between the categories. We therefore have enough evidence at a biological level to challenge the filter of gender polarization. The statement 'our anatomy is our destiny' suggests that the roles of males and females are determined by nature (biology) – they are not. If this were the case, then our society would be female-centred. To get a true sense of our destiny, we need to cleanse the doors of our perception from the effects of gender-coloured lenses.

Biologically, there is ample evidence to challenge the validity of applying the law of excluded middle. In the next chapter we will look at the topic of gender differences to discover whether the behaviour of women and men actually is so very different.

HUMAN ANATOMY QUIZ: ANSWERS

1. **False**. Men are biologically the weaker sex.
2. **False**. Men and women have the same hormones; it is only the relative levels that differ. Furthermore, men differ from other men and women differ from other women in terms of the levels of their hormones.
3. **True**. Women have testosterone.
4. **True**. The anus has an erotic capacity in all people, both men and women.
5. **True**. The anus has an erotic capacity irrespective of sexual orientation. Although for some people the sensations may be interpreted as pleasurable rather than as erotic.
6. **False**. The vagina is the birth canal; the collective term for the female sexual organs is the vulva.
7. **False**. A penis is an enlarged clitoris.
8. **True**. The clitoris is the only organ in the human body with the sole function of sexual pleasure.
9. **True**. The ovaries and the testes are formed from the same embryonic tissue.
10. **True**. Biologically the 'default' value of humans is female. This is why a penis is an enlarged clitoris and this is why men have nipples.
11. **False**. More accurately, men are women who made a bit of a detour (in the early stages of development).
12. **False**. From biological evidence the similarities between men and women are far greater than their differences.

Sex, Lies and Stereotypes

5

The Law of Averages and Educated Guesses: The Truth About Gender Differences

There are three kinds of lies: lies, damned lies and statistics
– Benjamin Disraeli, British politician (1804–81)

Statistics are like a bikini. What they reveal is suggestive, but what they conceal is vital – Aaron Levenstein, American modern-day politician

The fact that we are all human beings is infinitely more important than all the peculiarities that distinguish humans from one another – Simone de Beauvoir, French philosopher (1908–86)

PREVIEW

In this chapter we will:

* Review the psychology of gender differences and similarities.
* Discuss the problems of confusing what happens in the real world with what 'looks good on paper' in research.
* Discuss the effects of training on reducing gender differences
* Consider some guidelines for judging 'research', self-help books and pop-psychology books.

Shirts and blouses

Popular psychology and news items generalize from academic research in pursuit of a good headline. However, generalizations are made in academic psychology too. Research participants assigned to 'totally-male' or 'totally-female' groups are put there based solely on their outward appearance (shirts or blouses). And while baseline biological measures, such as blood tests for hormones and cheek swabs for chromosomes, are rarely used, biological conclusions are often reached. However, appearance is a social not a biological indicator. The very nature of scientific inquiry is often based on caution and conservatism; scientists are not supposed to go beyond the evidence. Outward appearance (gender identity) is not a reliable indicator of biological processes. So, until someone discovers a 'shirt and blouse desensitizing hormone', it makes sound scientific sense *not* to jump to biological conclusions based on social categories.

Vital statistics: proof or probability?

We also often read reports that science has 'proved' something or other. This is an overstatement. Evidence supports theories, it doesn't prove them. Evidence amasses slowly as studies are repeated. Even with the surest of concepts, there is always a chance that we may be wrong. Once upon a time the Earth was flat and the Sun orbited the Earth. Were they facts? No, they were theories and the evidence we had at the time supported them. Chance or probability is at the heart of scientific discovery. Our results aim to give us more confidence in theories, but the bottom line is that nothing is 100 per cent certain. We'll explore this point throughout this chapter.

Statistics are also a ubiquitous part of our lives. We cannot pick up a newspaper or magazine or watch a television programme without being bombarded by statistics in one form or another. Opinion polls and market research aim to represent our attitudes in the form of statistics. Indeed, we seem to place great value on these (seemingly) magical numbers. We buy moisturizers on the understanding that they will reduce fine lines by 40 per cent in six weeks. We even compare the odds of being struck by lightning with the odds of winning the lottery and yet still we gamble.

Such is our belief in an ordered and predictable universe that we believe even the fickle finger of fate must conform to some kind of pattern sooner or later. What we call the odds, science calls probability. Psychologists, much the same as bookmakers, like to calculate the odds too. Psychologists don't deal in absolute certainty, they work in the twilight worlds of probability, the law of averages and educated guesses. This hardly seems reassuring, but an understanding of the way psychologists work out the odds and the averages (statistics) is vital to our understanding of so-called gender differences.

Reports of research findings often conceal more that they reveal. Why? Because a cautious and accurate interpretation of the evidence rarely makes a good headline. Quite simply, we often read stories and draw conclusions that are not supported by the evidence. To explore this point I have developed a brief quiz on gender differences and similarities.

GENDER QUIZ: 'ALL OR SOMETHING'

On page 88 are 20 questions arranged in pairs. Each item deals with an aspect of human behaviour and experience in two slightly different ways. Some of the questions are about males and females (meaning girls and boys, men and women), other questions focus on adults and others focus on children of school age. In the tradition of the law of excluded middle, you should answer true or false to each question.

Please complete the quiz on page 88 before proceeding.

The main challenge of the quiz is to explore the difference between all and average. There is an important difference here and we will examine this throughout the chapter. There are also slight differences in the various terms for gender, such as male and female, boy and girl and man and woman.

Appreciating all of these differences will help you to develop critical thinking about gender issues. Sometimes even the most skilled researcher is not necessarily a skilled communicator. On the other hand, skilled communicators aren't necessarily skilled researchers. We often get the researcher's 'bottom line' through the filter of the entertaining headline and the subtleties of research are inevitably lost in translation. This happens in the popular press as well as in academic psychology.

Before we examine the questions from the quiz (the answers to which can be found on page 98), first let's consider the concept of 'difference'. As with most things, differences come in a range of sizes.

GENDER QUIZ: 'ALL OR SOMETHING'

1. On average, men can throw objects further than women can. **True or false?** _____

2. All men can throw further than all women can. **True or false?** _____

3. On average, females have better verbal abilities than males. **True or false?** _____

4. All females have better verbal abilities than all males. **True or false?** _____

5. On average, boys are better than girls in tests of mathematical ability. **True or false?** _____

6. All boys are better than all girls in tests of mathematical ability. **True or false?** _____

7. On average, females are more facially expressive when communicating than males. **True or false?** _____

8. All females are more facially expressive than all males when communicating? **True or false?** _____

9. On average, boys smile more than girls in social situations. **True or false?** _____

10. All boys smile more than all girls in social situations? **True or false?** _____

11. On average, men smile more in social situations than women? **True or false?** _____

12. All men smile more than all women in social situations. **True or false?** _____

13. On average, males are more aggressive than females. **True or false?** _____

14. All males are more aggressive than all females. **True or false?** _____

15. On average, men are more aggressive than women. **True or false?** _____

16. All men are more aggressive than all women. **True or false?** _____

17. On average, females show more helping behaviour than males. **True or false?** _____

18. All females show more helping behaviour than all males. **True or false?** _____

19. On average, men are more likely to approve of sexual intercourse without love than women? **True or false?** _____

20. All men approve of sex without love and all women disapprove. **True or false?** _____

Return to page 87.

Sex, Lies and Stereotypes

Different differences

I mentioned earlier that psychologists deal in probabilities; after all, they need some statistical calculations to try to rule out chance factors or errors that may have crept into the calculations. Psychologists work to tough odds: they have to be more than 95 per cent confident that their results do not occur due to chance or error, which equates to odds of more than 19:1 against. If their results meet stringent mathematical tests they can say that they have a 'statistically significant result'; this is different to how the word 'significant' is used in everyday language.

Now that's not the end of it. Just think of how many times you have read that a certain food is bad for you, only to read the following week that it's good for you. What should you believe? Science doesn't prove anything. Rather, sometimes evidence supports scientific theories and sometimes it doesn't: it depends what question the scientist is asking. So, how are we supposed to make sense of it all? Well, just like your average scientist, the average person is supposed to collect all the evidence 'for' and all the evidence 'against' and make an educated guess.

This seems like a lot of trouble for very little confidence. Statisticians recognize this and so devised a complex calculation called a meta-analysis. With this tool, the statistician is able to compare the results of many studies and provide an overall view: a bottom line. Thus a meta-analysis can help restore our confidence in scientific findings by removing a lot of the guesswork.

For the sake of simplicity, I am going to separate the gender differences into five main groups based on the possible scores from this calculation:

* Small.
* Small-to-moderate.
* Moderate.
* Moderate-to-large.
* Large.

In simple terms, meta-analysis compares the size of the differences between the overall average scores for women and men. Some of these differences will look good on paper *and* they will (probably) have some significance in the real world (the largest differences). The remainder are those that only a statistician would get excited over and would probably have little or no impact in the real world (the smaller differences).

Let's return to the All or Something gender quiz. For each case, I will indicate the size of the differences between men and women using the five categories. Those most likely to mean something in the real world are the large and moderate-to-large differences.

THROWING THINGS

We often hear that 'Men can throw further than women can', but is this true? Well, it sounds reasonable. For instance, we only have to watch the Olympic games to see how much further male athletes throw the javelin than female athletes for evidence of this fact. However, to get a more accurate picture, a scientist has to consider the evidence in a more logical way.

A scientist will take a group of men and a group of women and will calculate the average throwing distance for an object by both groups. However, if the average distance thrown by men is found to be further than that for women, this cannot be used as evidence that men throw further than women because the scientist still needs to apply the stringent statistical test to these figures to make sure they are truly representative. Even if the results for the group show that the average distance thrown by the males is greater than that by the females, some women may still have thrown further than some men.

If the scientist's original sample of people was representative of the population as a whole, they could begin to generalize their findings. They would probably find that while men can throw further than women, not all men can throw further than all women. This is a crucial distinction, but all too often it is one that is not made clear. True enough, the best throwers are more likely to be men and the less impressive throwers are more likely to be women. However, we are not dealing with absolutes here. The truth is that some women can throw further than can some men. These shades of grey in the middle cannot be excluded, but the truth gets in the way of a good story.

Similarly, psychology (science) is not conducted in a 'values vacuum'. Gender differences make good headlines so academic articles that show a gender difference rather than a similarity are more likely to get published by the news-hungry press. And, of course, academic psychology likes the exposure and excitement of a good headline too.

WORDS AND NUMBERS

Gender stereotyping dictates that women like to talk and that they talk more than men. This is linked to research on verbal ability and to differences between male and female brains. You may be led into thinking that if brain differences are found they must be as a result of large gender differences. However, if we examine the differences in average scores on verbal ability between males and females the differences are small. Females, on average, score only slightly higher than males. However, with such a very small difference, the degree of crossover (between the males and females) is much greater. There is a lot more 'middle' to exclude. Even if we focus solely on differences in grammar, the scores are only small-to-moderate.

Given that from an early age interactions with girl babies are more likely to be verbal, are we really surprised about gender difference? It is also true that if we practise something enough we can produce physical changes in the brain. This is how we learn. The small difference in verbal ability certainly doesn't prevent males from dominating conversations with females.

Traditionally, boys and girls were encouraged to study different subjects at school. Girls were encouraged in languages and the arts. Boys were encouraged in science and mathematics. Mathematical ability or 'being good with numbers' is something associated with the male gender stereotype. In fact, when comparing average scores, the differences are only small. Again, the crossover is far more noteworthy that the differences.

ON THE FACE OF IT

On average, women are more facially expressive when communicating than men. Furthermore, the difference this time is large. This still doesn't mean that all women are more facially expressive than all men. Again there is a degree of crossover. Nevertheless, boys are taught from an early age to suppress emotions, 'be brave' and to internalize the gender expectation that 'big boys don't cry'. However, looking at smiling in social situations, the results reveal that, on average, little boys smile slightly more (but the difference is tiny). Perhaps it is the greater likelihood that adults interact physically with baby boys, through tickling and the like.

Adult females on average smile more than adult males, and here the difference falls into the moderate-to-large range. Body language experts inform us that smiling is often used as a defensive gesture. It is possible that more direct avenues of communication may be denied to women. Smiles may simply be used to hide discomfort during conversation.

A BIT OF AGGRO

We often hear that men are more aggressive than women and that testosterone is to blame. This difference is so widely and frequently reported that we might conclude that it's a large gender difference. However, when average scores on various measures of aggression are analyzed, the difference is only a moderate one.

Expressed in everyday language, above average amounts of aggression are found in just over three out of five males. Whereas, above average amounts of aggression are found in about two in five females. This is a long way from the somewhat exaggerated claims. In fact, it has been calculated that gender only accounts for about five per cent of the variance in scores of aggression. In order words, 95 per cent of the differences in scores are explained by factors other than gender.

Aggression can be understood in the context of a number of factors, such as upbringing, situational factors, previous experience and so on. Those research findings are unlikely to make the headlines as they contradict expectations. Furthermore, the trend is towards reduced gender differences as we age. Looking at measures of aggression for adults, the differences in average scores between men and women are small-to-moderate.

In addition, according to gender-role stereotypes, females are more helpful than males. However, research shows that, on average, males are more likely to engage in helpful behaviour than females. But this is still only a small-to-moderate difference.

CASUAL SEX

Differences in physical ability aside, the largest gender differences lie in attitudes to sex. One of the most marked gender differences is around attitudes to casual sex and here the difference is large. On average, men are more likely to approve of penetrative intercourse without love than women are. However, men are only slightly more likely to approve of penetrative intercourse in a serious relationship than women are (small-to-moderate).

There are many fanciful theories as to why this might be. Most often we are told about maternal instincts, brain differences and the imperatives of the selection process. However, these theories rarely distinguish between reported attitudes (what people say they do) and actual behaviour (what they actually do). Nor do they mention the social opprobrium for a woman who makes it clear that she enjoys sex as much as a man. Biological theories never mention any social fear of being labelled a slut or a whore or the pride in being labelled a stud or stallion. The only organ of the human body solely for sexual pleasure, the clitoris, rarely gets a mention.

Personality and the law of the excluded middle

We saw in the previous chapter how personality traits are rarely all-or-nothing. Here are three diagrams that apply to any personality trait, such as aggression, decisiveness or activeness. They illustrate the law of excluded middle at work. In the first diagram we see the all-or-nothing approach.

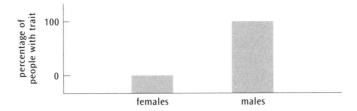

The above diagram creates the impression that we either possess the trait in abundance or that we don't possess it at all (either-or, all-or-nothing). In chapter 3 we discovered that this was untenable where you gave scores out of 100 for the various personality traits. Thus, instead of all-or-nothing we found that it's more accurate to assign percentage figures. A graph to illustrate this measure would look something like this:

You can see that only a few people have very weak (low) or very strong (high) scores. In the main we tend to cluster around the middle. However, when we look at separate graphs for males and females, and lay them one on top of the other the picture looks like this:

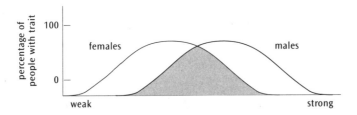

We can see from the diagram on the previous page that there is a degree of overlap, indicated by the grey area. It is this grey area that is often ignored or excluded when we take an all-or-nothing view. In many cases, this overlap (similarity) between the genders can be far greater than the differences. It is important to emphasize that with any personality trait (or ability) the debate is not *whether* there is a gender crossover, but *how much* of a crossover exits.

Training

Most observable gender differences fall in to the small-to-moderate range. In other words, although they are large enough to be noticed, they do not provide the basis for general statements. Looking at psychological evidence, gender differences have decreased over time, however what we are observing is not evolution but rather the effects of (long-term) training. After all, training is actually about taking the opportunity to change.

There have been enormous changes in the rights, roles and expectations of men and women since the 'halcyon' days of the 1950s. Social, political and economical factors have allowed women the opportunity to change and they have. Now you might say that some women haven't really changed and I agree. Of course not all women have changed in every way, but on average, they have.

The crucial factor is that people have had the opportunity to change and research has demonstrated that gender differences are highly susceptible to training. Put simply, the more you practise something, the more skilled you become. The good news is that the biggest changes are made in the early stages. So the small-to-moderate gender differences can be eliminated quite quickly.

Most barriers to change are: existing cultural and social expectations; opportunities to learn through, for example, the toys we get as children; the subject choices available at school; the division of labour; and gender-role expectations. All of which prove that inherent ability is not the issue – it's the social context.

Smoke and mirrors

There are numerous articles, books, websites and television programmes that claim to address gender roles and relationships. But behind the

 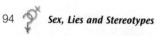

snappy titles, the headlines and the spin, they often tend to be variations on the same pop-psychology theme and that when research evidence is included it has often passed its sell-by date: it's old news.

Research that supports the 'different planet' view is reported uncritically, while anything that challenges the 'battle of the sexes' view is generally ignored. There is a wealth of research by the leading lights in the fields of sex, gender and sexuality that never finds its way into popular sources.

As we've been talking about raising the stakes, here are a few tips to help you appraise, more critically, the information that you see and hear about sex, gender and relationships.

BE SCEPTICAL

Often what you see and hear in newspapers and magazines is purely for entertainment. If it offers simplistic advice or information, then you probably aren't being told the whole story. Does the sample appear representative? Do they discuss findings in terms of 'all' or 'on average'? Just how large is the difference (or similarity)?

SEEK OUT THE ORIGINAL SOURCES AND ADDITIONAL INFORMATION

Check out references to other sources. You may have a different take on the evidence and reach different conclusions, so seek out evidence for alternative viewpoints from books or the internet, particularly if the material appears to lack a balanced view.

Never take things at face value.

LOOK OUT FOR THE FILTERS, LENSES AND STEREOTYPES

Hopefully you are now more aware of the filters through which we view the world. Beware of the simple link between genital shape and personality. Beware of material that only considers extremes and tries to present a black-and-white picture. Remember the law of excluded middle. Look out for what may be concealed not just what is revealed.

In other words, read between the lines and look for biases: is the material heavily inclined to a particular view?

BEWARE OF HIDDEN AGENDAS

Does the author imply you are a deviant or morally deficient for seeing the world in unorthodox or different ways? Does the research have a political or religious agenda? Is it 'sponsored' by an organization? If so, does this 'sponsorship' bias the interpretation of the evidence?

Many public relations (PR) companies have picked up on the idea that 'research' sells. So beware of 'startling new research' that suggests your life could be enhanced by buying a particular product.

WHAT IS RESEARCH?

The word research is used in many contexts. People may refer to a brief period of internet exploration as research, while others do research that has been commissioned to support an advertising campaign. Research conducted for a television programme is different to academic research, which is conducted according to ethical guidelines and undergoes a peer-review process (i.e. it is scrutinized by other academics before it is published).

As a general rule, research should be something you can obtain along with the credentials of the researcher. If they claim to have a PhD., you should be able to get a copy of it. For instance, copies of PhDs given at British Universities are held at the British Library (mine included). It may seem a little depressing, but it's true to say that we can't trust all sources of evidence and so it's worth checking out the credentials of the researcher. The PhD. thesis represents the 'original contribution to knowledge' that entitles the author to call himself or herself a doctor. A contribution to knowledge means at the very least that the doctor has research skills. If you can't find evidence of a doctor's contribution to knowledge than you have every right to be suspicious of their credentials.

THE CULT OF THE EXPERT

The Western world's preoccupation with celebrity has also seen a rise in the cult of the celebrity. Routinely, some so-called experts will happily speculate on the inner workings of the celebrity mind. However, guidelines from many professiona bodies, such as the British Psychological Society, make it clear that their members should not discuss the lives of celebrities as it is unethical. neither should experts talk outiosde of their area of expertise. For instance, if an expert has a PhD. in the psychological effects of dandruff they are hardly qualified to discuss the personal lives of the latest diva. Selling insurance policies door-to-door may give you an invaluable insight into people's behaviour, but it doesn't make you a psychologist, just as owning a craft knife doesn't make you a surgeon.

In the area of gender and sexuality there are plenty of 'experts'. However, on close inspection some of these experts are only actually offering home-spun philosophy gained from the 'University of Life'. Of course, everyone is entitled to their opinion; however, more often than not those opinions are based on limited and outdated knowledge and hence belong more to the 'Kindergarten of the Stereotype'. Beware of anyone who begins a statement with the words 'As we all know…'; it should start 'As evidence shows…'.

Conclusion: What's the difference?

In the last two chapters we have considered the biological, physical and psychological differences between men and women. So let's add a few more questions to the All or Something gender quiz on page 88:

21. All men and all women are so different that they may as well be from different planets? **True or false?** _____
22. Some men seem to be from different planets to women, in some situations, at least some of the time. **True or false?** _____
23. The filters with which we view the roles of men, women and relationships affect our perception of them? **True or false?** _____
24. Men and women are more similar than they are different. **True or false?** _____

We have found that there are some psychological differences between women and men. However, only a few of these have any great impact in the real world. Even then they can be reduced or eliminated by training. Although not exactly lies, much of what we read about gender differences has more to do with half-truths than real truths. Often what the statistics reveal is not as important as what they conceal. Again, we see the law of excluded middle in action. As with biology, we are more alike than different.

In the next chapter, we are going to advance the argument one step further. We may consider gender-role stereotypes to be harmless ideals to which we should all aspire, but is living our lives according to the 'oughts' and 'shoulds' of fixed gender roles actually harmful to both our physical and mental health?

GENDER QUIZ: *ANSWERS*

1. **True** (large difference). On average men can throw futher than can women.
2. **False**. There is a degree of crossover.
3. **True** (small difference). On average, females score higher than males do on measures of verbal ability.
4. **False**. There is a degree of crossover.
5. **True** (small difference). On average, boys score higher than girls do on measures of mathematical ability.
6. **False**. There is a degree of crossover.
7. **True** (large difference). On average, women are more facially expressive when communicating than men are.
8. **False**. There is a degree of crossover.
9. **True** (small difference). On average, boys smile more in social situations than girls do.
10. **False**. There is a degree of crossover.
11. **False**. On average, women smile more in social situations than men do (moderate-to-large difference).
12. **False**. There is a degree of crossover.
13. **True** (moderate difference). On average males score higher on measures of aggression than females do.
14. **False**. There is a degree of crossover.
15. **True** (small-to-moderate difference). On average, men score higher on measures of aggression than women do.
16. **False**. There is a degree of crossover.
17. **False**. On average, males are more likely to engage in helping behaviour than females are (small-to-moderate difference).
18. **False**. There is a degree of crossover.
19. **True** (large difference). On average, males are more likely than females are to approve of sexual intercourse without love.
20. **False**. There is a degree of crossover.

Note: For items 21 to 24: you can decide for yourself.

Sex, Lies and Stereotypes

6

WARNING: Gender-Role Stereotypes May Be Bad for Your Health

The more we rigidly define ourselves, the less likely we are able to cope with the infinite variety of life – Ernest Rossi, modern-day psychobiologist

We forfeit three-quarters of ourselves to be like other people – Arthur Schopenhauer, German philosopher (1788–1960)

One's only real life is the life one never leads– Oscar Wilde, Irish writer (1854–1900)

PREVIEW

In this chapter we will:

* Review material from psychology and studies of lifestyle and health behaviours relating to gender roles.
* Argue that living our lives according to the rigid gender-role. stereotypes of 'real men' and 'real women' can be harmful to both our physical and mental health.
* Consider the benefits of androgyny and partnership.

Zero-sum game

As soon as young children realize their gender is not going to change they really get into the whole gender identity thing. On one level it's all a bit of a game. It is about dressing up, belonging to the 'right' group and doing the 'right' thing. Exaggerating the extreme points at the ends of the continuum is about creating clear boundaries. As we have discussed, play-acting helps make the world a more predictable place. However, children's games usually have an end point. The gender game doesn't.

We often hear people say, it's not the winning that counts but the taking part. The gender game is all about taking part – 'all the world's a stage and we are the players'. Like method actors, we 'lose ourselves', playing out typecast roles in a lifelong soap opera. Now, if you argue that the gender story is told from the perspective of the male leading role, it suggests that the male lead in the gender soap opera always gets the highest pay, the best perks and the most power. In real life though, while it is true that gender is based on a male perspective and that women are disadvantaged socially and economically, we cannot necessarily assume that everything that is good for men is automatically bad for women. Indeed, we could also argue that improvements in conditions for women must be to the detriment of men. In this case, gender is viewed as a zero-sum (all-or-nothing) game in which one gender can only benefit at the expense of the other. This has serious implications for relationships.

Throughout the book we have considered how often the differences within each of the categories of men and women may be greater than the differences between the two categories. A large component of 'true masculinity' is related to competition and superiority: it's about one's place in the power structure. This means that men are in direct competition with other men. We can therefore conclude that the gender-role stereotype of 'true masculinity', with 'winner takes all', is not necessarily good for all men. Rather than gender stereotypes being a convenient way of making sense of the world, we have a model of gender that only benefits a minority.

The goal of a zero-sum game of gender is to provide certainty, but what are the penalties? We are constantly haunted by the burden of expectations and of living up to impossible ideals. Perhaps it is not surprising that researchers are increasingly attributing both physical and mental health problems to rigid gender roles. So, being 'real men' or 'real women' may actually be bad for our health.

Sex, Lies and Stereotypes

Three little words

There are three little words by which we measure our worth, give our life meaning and help to make the world a more predictable place. No, not 'I love you', but: 'ought', 'should' and 'must'.

'Ought', 'should' and 'must' are words by which we communicate the expectation of gender roles. Men and women *ought* to think in particular ways: real men are 'strong and tough' and 'only the best is good enough'. Girls and boys *should* behave in particular ways: big boys don't cry and little girls should be 'ladylike'. Males and females *must* follow the 'oughts' and 'shoulds' to the letter as traditional roles and family values are based on rigid black-and-white categories.

Poor mental health is associated with this lack of autonomy or control over one's life. It is recognized in therapy, counselling and coaching circles that living one's life according to the inflexible backdrop of 'oughts', 'musts' and 'shoulds' is a contributing factor for emotional and mental distress. The solution to such distress often focuses on challenging rigid and inflexible thinking and behaviour. Because, although on one level black-and-white thinking may help to provide structure and reduce uncertainty, it can also be counterproductive when taken to extremes. The black-and-white categories of gender stereotypes are often at odds with the fuzzy boundaries and shades of grey in the real world. Coping often equates to flexible thinking.

In chapter 3 we looked at the pillars of 'true womanhood' and 'true manhood'. For women the emphasis is on fitting in within a male-centred world and putting the needs of others before their own. For men, the emphasis is on being better than others, suppressing weakness and judging personal worth in terms of external rewards. Girls learn early on to attune to and accept the needs of others. Boys learn to become more individuated and status conscious. Females are encouraged to focus on the personal, males on the positional. Many of the roles and expectations and psychological traits attached to stereotypical masculinity, such as aggressiveness, ambition, success, striving, virility, asceticism and competitiveness, are intrinsically tied to men's preoccupation with power over others and attempts to impose their value system on others. With stereotypical femininity, the focus for women is on submission and support.

Gender as a performance is an ongoing work-in-progress rather than something intrinsic to our being. If we consider the art of acting and performance it is simultaneously about light and shadow: actors illuminate the role while concealing their real selves. However, actors can remove the costumes and make-up, but people can't remove their gender (at least, not easily). Like actors, if we play our gender-role stereotypes well, we can attain 'rave reviews' of social approval. But even when we do not conform to them, they affect us directly as standards of behaviour.

The opening quotes are all concerned with the costs of not living one's 'real' life. Research shows that conforming rigidly to stereotypes has a negative effect on psychological well-being. Let's consider the cost of living up to these expectations.

Exercise: Comfort-zones

Chapter 3 explored the tenability of rigid gender roles and the extent to which our gender is dependent on a situation. However, we did not consider the degree to which you are comfortable in expressing various personality traits. This is addressed in the following exercise.

Using a scale from 0 to 100, answer the following question for all of the traits; zero indicates you are 'not at all comfortable' and 100 means you are completely (100 per cent) comfortable. Use any whole number in the range to indicate your degree of comfort.

How comfortable do you feel in situations that require you to be:

_____ Powerful	_____ Strong	_____ Active
_____ Competent	_____ Goal-oriented	_____ Independent
_____ Efficient	_____ Assertive	_____ Competitive
_____ Logical	_____ Adventurous	_____ Ambitious
_____ Dominant	_____ Tough	_____ Decisive
_____ Emotional	_____ Nurturing	_____ Co-operative
_____ Intuitive	_____ Passive	_____ Sensitive
_____ Submissive	_____ Compassionate	_____ Tender
_____ Talkative	_____ Gentle	_____ Tactful
_____ Helpful	_____ Relationship-oriented	_____ Concerned about appearance

CALCULATE YOUR ROLE FLEXIBILITY QUOTIENT (RFQ)

* Make sure that you have scores for all of the personality traits.
* Add up the scores and divide by 30.
* The answer is your RFQ: _____

For the sake of simplicity (again) we will use the mid-point as the cut-off.

* Scores of 51 and above are considered higher scores.
* Scores of 50 or lower are considered lower scores.

Higher RFQ

Overall, this score indicates that you have a broader comfort zone and therefore a higher degree of behavioural and emotional flexibility across a wider range of situations and with a wider variety of people. It indicates that you are comfortable with the whole of the human experience.

Lower RFQ

Overall, this score indicates that you have a narrower comfort zone and therefore a lower degree of behavioural and emotional flexibility. Your degree of comfort may be strongly dependent on situations or particular groups of people. You may only be comfortable expressing traits associated with one of the gender stereotypes.

Over-identification with gender-role stereotypes restricts the emotional and behavioural repertoire of an individual. In many ways the male role is more restrictive than the female role. 'Sissy' behaviour for boys is more likely to receive condemnation at an earlier age than 'tomboy' behaviour is for girls. For females, the pressures to conform are not intense until adolescence. Little girls engaging in rough and tumble play are considered endearing. However, boys who show tender feelings, such as playing with dolls are more likely to meet with disapproval. Thus boys inherit a greater anxiety when aspects of their behaviour are considered feminine. Anti-femininity ('no girly stuff') is one of the four pillars of the male gender-role stereotype. Some psychologists argue that early experiences of disapproval associated with 'girly stuff' (femininity) become deeply ingrained in the male psyche and form the basis of misogyny.

Chapter 3 looked at four gender types: androgynous, masculine, feminine and undifferentiated.

Masculine-type people tend to show higher degrees of comfort and competence for tasks that require assertiveness and independence, such as taking the lead in a group situation. Such tasks and situations are called instrumental tasks. Men stereotypically embody instrumentality and are task-oriented.

Feminine-type people tend to show higher degrees of comfort and competence in tasks requiring nurturance and empathy, such as looking after a pet. Such tasks are called expressive tasks. Women stereotypically embody expressiveness and are emotion-oriented.

Androgynous-type people show competence and comfort in both expressive and instrumental tasks.

Undifferentiated-type people lack competence and are uncomfortable across a broad range of tasks and behaviours. However, as with all areas of human behaviour and experience, there is a large degree of crossover. It is therefore possible to have socially masculine-type biological women and socially feminine-type biological women, and it is the same for men.

Research shows that men with high-masculinity scores experience discomfort and anxiety when required to perform tasks, roles and behaviours that are considered expressive because such things are deemed feminine. Similarly women with high femininity scores experience discomfort when required to perform tasks, roles and behaviours that are considered instrumental because such things are deemed masculine.

Early learning experiences, our upbringing, our schooling and our peer-group all help to shape our attitudes to gender roles. In this way, many of us learn from a young age to internalize the expectation that crossing gender boundaries will have a negative consequence. By contrast, androgynous-type people have enjoyed greater opportunity to express a broad spectrum of emotions and experiences. Consequently, they are less likely to use gender lenses to process the world around them, responding instead to the demands of the situation. Androgynous types are also less likely to expect negative consequences as a result of crossing gender roles and therefore enjoy greater flexibility and freedom in their experiences.

Rigid adherence to (stereotypical) gender roles narrows human experience and hinders opportunity. While gender roles may create clear boundaries and thus make the world a simpler place to understand, they also create barriers to leading a fuller life. Why settle for half the human experience?

Sex, Lies and Stereotypes

The half-life of stress

The film *Pleasantville* (1998) documents the changes that occur in a 1950s fictional soap-opera town as a result of the influence of two late-20th-century teenagers. Sexual awakening and the transgression of appropriate gender-typed behaviour are marked with a change from black and white to Technicolor in the film. However, for the people in the town of Pleasantville, the changes rocked the very foundations of their lives. In this new world, the husband returning home from work finds his customary cheery greeting 'Hi honey, I'm home' met with silence. There is no perfectly presented, smiling wife to meet him with a hot meal. So, in disbelief he sits at the dining table until dark, waiting for normality to return.

Now imagine two people, a typical woman and a typical man, cryogenically frozen in the 1950s and then revived in the 21st century. Would they be able to contemplate the technological advances? Would they be able to cope with the significant changes in gender roles or would they quickly perish from the stress of such an alien world? We often mistakenly assume that 'survival of the fittest' means 'survival of the physically strongest and aggressive'. It doesn't. Instead it relates to the survival of those who are most adaptable to change. Living a half-life is not adaptive. Just like the characters in *Pleasantville* who found it difficult to adapt or the cryogenically frozen couple, those people living a half-life are also more likely to experience stress.

A crucial feature of anxiety or stress is increased physiological arousal. If this level is maintained in the long term this can lead to health problems. There are three stages in our physiological response to stress: alarm, resistance and exhaustion.

In the alarm stage our body's fight or flight responses are activated. Physiological changes equip us to deal with a threat, whether it be a surge of strength to put up a fight or a surge of speed to help us to run away. Initially, stress triggers an increase in our heart rate, blood pressure and respiration (breathing rate), extra sugar is released into the bloodstream and we sweat more. The release of the hormone adrenaline perpetuates this state of heightened arousal or readiness.

In the resistance stage, if the stressor is not removed, some of these responses decrease in intensity although we still maintain a state of readiness. However, if we remain in the alarm stage for long periods of time, the high levels of adrenaline contribute to depressing our body's immune responses and we become more vulnerable to viruses and colds. However, stress has been implicated in health problems that are far more serious.

For the majority of people, the stressor is dealt with in the first two stages, allowing the bodily responses to return to normal. In extreme cases exhaustion occurs, where there is a depletion of the body's resources.

The RFQ provides an indicator of how comfortable you may feel across a variety of situations. In theory, the lower the score, the greater your discomfort. Therefore, if you are required to respond across a spectrum of emotional and behavioural situations, you may experience mild anxiety or stress. Androgynous types (those who are more flexible and less gender-stereotyped), therefore, have an advantage.

There are also differences between men and women when it comes to some of the more serious mental health problems, suggesting a negative influence from gender-role stereotypes. Problems most common to women include anxiety disorders and depression. Stereotypically, women are socialized to be more fearful (and in need of protection) than men are, and it is perhaps not surprising that they are more likely to suffer from phobias. As 'slimness' is part of idealized femininity, eating disorders are also more common in women. As the male stereotype emphasizes independence and dominance, it is not surprising that men are more prone to more 'active' disorders, such as substance abuse, gambling, pyromania and antisocial personality disorders.

Men are more likely to externalize their negative feelings and become aggressive, whereas women are more likely to internalize their negative feelings resulting in negative attitudes to their bodies and self criticism. Men take it out on others whereas women take it out on themselves. In both cases, we can relate these tendencies to gender-role stereotypes; where men are socialized to be hell-raisers, tough guys and big-shots, women are socialized to put the needs of others before their own.

In the previous two chapters we discussed the biological and psychological similarity of women and men. However, we also discovered that women are biologically the stronger sex. So, what part does biology play in health differences between women and men?

Nature versus nurture

Biologically, females have some slight advantage over males. As mentioned, males are more susceptible to a range of hereditary diseases and conditions because of the weaker male (Y) chromosome. Stillbirth and infant mortality are also greater for males. Males, on average, also have a lower life expectancy than females. Estimates vary, but the overall world average amounts to between three and four years. In the developed world, the female 'advantage' is around seven or eight years. In Eastern Europe it is around 11 years.

Although the differences look quite large for women and men at first glance, when other research variables are controlled the difference narrows. Factors such as age and employment status tend to increase the differences in life expectancy. For instance, in Australia the difference between indigenous men and non-indigenous women can be as much as 23 years. Clearly social, economic and political factors have an effect on life expectancy.

In support of this, when we examine gender differences in health in controlled environments we see that they are less pronounced than in the general population. For example in a kibbutz (an Israeli commune), where there are less marked gender divisions of labour, there are no significant health differences between women and men. In a long-term psychiatric hospital where the environment is more controlled, men and women have roughly similar health expectations. Under such circumstances the incidence of, say, heart disease between men and women is very similar – even though in the general population men are almost four times more likely to suffer from heart disease than women.

Overall, research indicates that difference in health status (between men and women) relates more to social differences in lifestyle than to underlying biological vulnerability.

The rising cost of living up to expectations

Masculinity is not necessarily good for men. True 'manhood' requires men to constantly evaluate themselves to reach external standards. It's all about measuring up in terms of physical size and toughness, status and competition. From an early age boys are encouraged to display their muscles. They strive for size and strength and, for many men, masculinity equals muscularity. Bodybuilders put their health at risk by over-training, going on extremely low-calorie diets, and sometimes using steroids. Some writers have even suggested that bodybuilding is about men transforming themselves into living, hard-veined phallic symbols.

The cardinal aspiration of the hellraiser means that men are more likely than women to engage in risky behaviour, such as smoking, drinking, dangerous driving and acts of aggression. Consequently, men tend to be involved in more fatal accidents and are more likely to be murdered than women. Male violence in one area of life tends to spill over into others. In terms of sexual relationships, men tend to have more sexual partners, yet, worryingly, are more likely to trick or force people to have sex with them. Men are also more likely to show violence towards partners. High scores on measures of masculinity are strongly related to higher measures of mistrust and of hostility to other people. 'Real men' are supposed to suppress their emotions or any aspect of their behaviour that might be considered feminine ('no girly stuff'). Even examining one's own testicle can be considered an 'un-masculine' thing to do, so some men needlessly die of testicular cancer as a result of this conditioning.

It is important to emphasize at this point that we are discussing masculinity and its performance and not men as such. It is not who men are but how they are socialized to behave. Even suicide highlights a gender difference. Although women are more likely to attempt suicide, men are more likely to succeed. It's sad to see that, according to the stereotype, 'real' men are not supposed to fail, not even when trying to kill themselves. Of course, not all men are the same. Not all men share the same stakes in the gender order. For every Top Dog (one of the pillars of 'true manhood') there has to be an underdog.

One of the four pillars of 'true womanhood' is the symbol of the good girl/nice girl. She looks after her body and watches what she eats. Therefore, perhaps unsurprisingly, women are more likely to embrace healthier lifestyles. Women, on average, are also more likely to seek help for emotional and physical problems.

Mainly due to social constraints, women's tobacco use and alcohol consumption were traditionally lower than men's . However, with changes in the role of women in society have come changes in alcohol and tobacco use by women. In fact, it is young women rather than young men who are now taking up smoking. Thus, one sign of gender equality is the regrettable rise in deaths from lung cancer among women.

Although women, on average, have a higher life expectancy than men, women seem to have poorer health overall. They access more health services and medications and also undergo more surgical procedures. Women usually visit the doctor for help with psychological problems and weight gain and for general examinations and conditions related to their reproductive systems.

Women tend to suffer from more serious conditions later in life than men. Men are more likely to report ulcers, asthma, stomach symptoms, eye

Sex, Lies and Stereotypes

complaints, cardiovascular problems and hypertension before the age of 60, whereas women are more likely to seek medical attention for diabetes, anaemia, rheumatoid arthritis, lupus, respiratory and gastrointestinal problems, Alzheimer's disease and hypertension after the age of 60. Overall, trends suggest that women's more frequent visits to the doctor's surgery may prevent problems from becoming serious.

The benefits of a more androgynous approach to gender in the context of coronary heart disease (CHD) are clear. Stereotypically, men's diets have a higher ratio of saturated to polyunsaturated fats and lower vitamin C intake. Such diets are associated with CHD. However, generally men engage in more physical exercise than women, which should reduce their chances of CHD. Thus a combination of the healthier diet of women and the healthier exercise regime of men would result in a much healthier lifestyle overall. This is just one example of a marriage of lifestyle approaches through which both men and women may benefit.

Dearly beloved

Long-term relationships are related positively to physical and mental health for men and women. However, the benefit for men is greater. Both men and women in long-term relationships live longer than single people. They also tend to lose fewer days from work and visit the doctor less. Some research has looked at the life expectancy of men and women in their mid-40s to mid-50s, with and without (that is, single, widowed or divorced) partners.

The results showed that of men aged 45–54 years without a partner 6 out of 25 would die within ten years, compared to only 3 in 25 of men with a partner. However, for women aged 45–54 years without a partner, 2 in 25 would die within 10 years compared to 1 in 25 of those with a partner. Figures for mental health also show a similar pattern. Although being in a relationship (married) is beneficial for both men and women, it clearly has greater benefits for men.

Being married or in a relationship often has the economic benefits of an increased income, but research indicates that an extra benefit to men is a healthier lifestyle and a larger social network. Relationships are more beneficial for women when they are more democratic. Women tend to be healthier when there is a greater equality in decision making than in relationships that are more male-dominated. A greater emphasis on partnership appears to create a win-win situation, especially as more equal relationships do not negatively affect men's health.

The worst health conditions are reported for unemployed men who are in a relationship with children. Arguably, this is because they are denied the stereotypical 'breadwinner' role. For men, negative health implications may be associated with the traditional male gender-role stereotype. At mid-life, women who have followed the traditional 'housewife' role have poorer health than peers who have followed a less traditional (stereotyped) route.

Overall, relationships are more beneficial for men and to a certain extent serve to reduce the impact of the hazardous traditional male role. In many ways we have started to enjoy greater equality in relationships as we move towards a model of partnership. Relationships need not be a zero-sum game in which one partner benefits at the expense of the other. Women may benefit from relationships that are more democratic, but this does not have a negative impact on men. In true partnerships, both are winners.

Conclusion: Sex, drag and rockin' roles

Everyday language suggests that we recognize and even accept different kinds of male and female roles, so isn't it time we looked for new models of relating to each other that are more in tune with modern life? We often talk about 'new men' and then mistakenly describe them as being 'in touch with their feminine side'. This perpetuates the myth that men and women are radically different. We aren't. Instead we could consider talking about men getting in touch with their 'expressive side' or 'nurturing side'. Women could be described as getting in touch with their 'instrumental side' or 'assertive side'. It still suggests an artificial division between human qualities, but at least we have taken gender out of the equation. More accurately we could talk about more being rounded and grounded human beings – this is what androgyny means.

As we have seen in previous chapters, the world is largely viewed from a male perspective and therein lies the imbalance of power. But in many ways, this just makes it even more difficult for men to adopt characteristics that are considered feminine. It's something of a bitter irony that according to the stereotype, men are supposed to be survivors. The sad fact is that they aren't, and they don't! We have already opened dialogue on the 'nature' of masculinity. If the traditional brand of masculinity is bad for

Sex, Lies and Stereotypes

men, women and society then maybe masculinity is long overdue for a re-brand. Maybe we need a new improved formula.

In many ways the 'stay at home' woman was a product of Victorian values and aspirations. As a wife, she was a middle-class status symbol and a measure of affluence. So femininity also needs re-branding. At the heart of the cardinal aspiration of 'no girly stuff' is the assumption that femininity is inferior. Implicit within the female gender stereotype (and the four virtues of 'true womanhood') is the deference to others, usually men. Overall, women's lower status and lesser power in society mean they have less control over their lives. They are more likely to live in an unpredictable environment but within paradoxically rigid gender roles, which are in turn supposed to make the world a more predictable place. Whereas rigid roles do provide a stronger sense of structure they also bring predictable forfeiture. There are costs. Predictability may mean comfort at some level but inevitably restrictions limit choices, which ultimately brings discomfort.

The traditional power structure in relationships is not inevitable. The gender division of personality traits and emotions is arbitrary. We have chosen artificial black-and-white predictability over the fuzzy boundaries that naturally exist. Living in the shadow of gender 'ideals' means that we never live life to the full. We need expressive, nurturing men; we need assertive, instrumental women; we need to live the whole of the human experience. Rather than a zero-sum game, we need a win-win situation.

And so we conclude that the second part of this book has taken a brief journey back to basics. Far from inevitable, our gender roles are mainly socially constructed. They represent the structure by which we attempt to make sense of the world. However, as we have seen, in terms of our biology, our psychology and our health, gender roles make very little sense. Our everyday references to 'new men', 'new women' and 'relationships based on partnership' are signs that we need to move beyond a black-and-white view. We have considered enough evidence in this book to at least think about entertaining other views. Just like the charcters in *Pleasantville*, we may just about be ready to burst into colour. Let's see.

PART THREE

Changing Views:
Colour Vision

7

Down to Earth: Co-operation Not Alien-Nation

I don't know why people are afraid of new ideas. I am terrified of the old ones – John Cage, American composer (1912–92)

The problems that exist in the world today cannot be solved by the level of thinking that created them – Albert Einstein, physicist (1879–1955)

No one sews a piece of new cloth on an old garment; if he does, the patch tears away from it, the new from the old, and a worse tear is made. And no one puts new wine into old wineskins; if he does, the wine will burst the skins, and the wine is lost, and so are the skins; but new wine is for fresh skins – Mark 21-22; BIBLE (Revised Standard Version, 1956)

PREVIEW

In this chapter we will:

* Return to the mythology of New Sineplia..
* Examine the scriptural story of Adam and Eve and assumptions about hunter-gatherers.
* Consider partnership views of relationships.

Return to New Sineplia

We left the inhabitants of New Sineplia in a state of discontent. They had forgotten they were supposed to be different until a scholar from old Sineplia wrote a book to remind everyone (mainly the Anigavlians) of their respective places in the grand scheme of things. They attempted to rekindle their old identities. At first this was easy. They exaggerated their roles like school children let loose on the dressing up box. Of course, the Sineplians didn't change very much at all. This was mainly to do with the self-help manual which was Sineplian-centric, that is, it was written from a Sineplian viewpoint. A number of Anigavlians (yes, the pesky bookish ones) decided to conduct their own research. They called their school of thought Anigavlianism. These scholars soon began to piece together an alternative perspective. Predictably, the Sineplians accused them of being too subjective. Undeterred, they carried on with their research and argued that 'objectivity' was the word Sineplian's used to describe their own subjectivity. The Sineplians plumbed the depths of their collective psyche and fired back the razor-sharp witty riposte: 'Shut up you ugly old Sineplian-haters.' Ah! There's nothing like a logical and well-reasoned argument.

The research of the Anigavlian scholars led to the discovery of several lesser-known ancient texts, hidden away for centuries, most notably the *Mons Veneris*. It told of a time before the great earthquake when all people lived in harmony and partnership in the land of Genitalia. When a great canyon appeared in the land some interpreted it as a sign from one of their gods. The fear of further retribution caused them to abandon all gods except the powerful one. Superstition caused some of the Genitalians to persecute all those who clung to the old ways. The people on the one side of the canyon flung the evil-doers into the abyss. On the other side, those who wished to distance themselves from the evil-doers, flung themselves into the abyss. After considerable flinging (both voluntary and forced), by chance the Genitalians had sorted themselves into two distinct types of people. On one side of Mother Nature's Crevice (later renamed 'The Great Divide'), stood the spear wavers and on the other the basket weavers. Of course, the spears of the Sineplians, being scientifically minded, eventually became light-sabres. The Anigavlians held on to their baskets. Eventually they drifted inland and forgot about the existence of the people on the other side, helped along by a bout of viral amnesia. That would have been the end had the Anigavlian scholars not discovered an even more obscure text, one that had been ignored for aeons.

Sex, Lies and Stereotypes

The *Glans Clitoridis* had been revealed to an Anigavlian scholar in a dream in which she, in the form of a dove, had looked down upon the Great Divide. The world looked very different from the air than it did from the average Genitalian back garden. The scholar could see that the edges of the cavity did not extend across the land but became progressively narrower. Finally, the edges met at a sacred carved wooden monument dedicated to sacred sexual pleasure, where people lived and loved together in partnership and harmony, celebrating their common origin as they had done from the beginning of time.

Of course, the Sineplian scholars scoffed at this utopian view and contended that the sacred monument was nothing but an inferior, primitive, pale imitation of their tall towers. They maintained that their explorers had also ventured along the edge of the Great Divide (albeit in the opposite direction) and all they found was a cesspit!

THE DIRECTOR'S CUT

We've probably all seen a movie that is re-released at a later date labelled 'the director's cut'. For the director it represents a restoration of the original vision, often longer and more complex. The new cut may restore footage of characters and scenes that ended up on the cutting room floor. Inevitably, the director had to pay lip service to many significant parties. Movies aren't only artistic visions, they have economic prospects, too. It's all too easy to think that the 'movie' of gender has been told in its entirety but, as we have learnt, it has not. Social, economic and political obligations have resulted in a limited black-and-white print, mainly because of the significant cuts to the interesting stuff in the middle.

Much of the material in this book is like the footage that's left on the cutting room floor. The story of gender, up until this point, has only been shown in black and white: the new footage is in glorious Technicolor. In this book we have also stripped away much of the 'Hollywood-type' gloss. In many instances we've gone right back to the book.

In chapter 4 we returned to the biology books and discovered that the filter of gender stereotypes distorted early 'scientific' views of 'The Egg and Sperm Race'. The egg and the sperm work in partnership to build a bridge. It's a co-operative process not an antagonistic one. If you think of them having a common goal, then it makes sense.

If we really must do things by the book, then let's go back to the Garden of Eden to reconsider the prototypical model of relationships.

Other halves

I became interested in the story of Adam and Eve after reading a justification for homophobia by an American evangelist who said: 'If God had meant people to be gay he would have created Adam and Steve, not Adam and Eve.' In short, heterosexuality and male domination are supposedly God's will and that's the end of the debate. However, simply re-reading the account of creation in Genesis casts doubt on this view. In Genesis 1:26-27, we read:

> 26: Then God said, 'Let us make man in **our** image, after **our** likeness; and let them have dominion over the fish of the sea, and over the birds of the air, and over the cattle, and over all the earth, and over every creeping thing that creeps upon the earth.'
> 27: So God created man in his own image, in the image of God he created him; **male and female he created them**.

I have emphasized (in bold) some of the words in the text. What's all this about *our* image and *our* likeness? This makes God sound plural. The phrase, 'male and female he created them' can be read in two ways. Either God has created two separate beings, one male and one female, or else God has created one being, comprising maleness and femaleness. As Adam and Eve didn't appear until the second chapter of Genesis, the second option seems more feasible. The original being was a hermaphrodite. It was both male and female. From this we can infer that the first being was psychologically androgynous. However, more importantly, if the first being was created in God's image, then surely God must have been androgynous too?

Maybe something got lost in the translation. The word for God (*elohim*), in this instance, could be interpreted as a plural form. Although 'Adam' is often translated as a man's name, in Hebrew it could mean man or mankind (plural). It is a generic term for humans and denotes our (supposed) origin literally from red earth. Admittedly, the exhortation to 'be fruitful and multiply' (Genesis 1:28) suggests that 'it' or 'they' were able to reproduce, but given that they are not human in the sense we understand it today, we need not infer sexual intercourse.

It was later in Genesis 2:18, that the gods acknowledged the original human was lonely and made a helper fit for 'him'. Not surprisingly there has been some debate regarding the status of this helper. It is commonly interpreted as a helper of lower status. However the Hebrew word for helper (*ezer*) was used

⚥ *Sex, Lies and Stereotypes*

elsewhere to describe God or the gods. The word translated as 'fit' (*kenegdo*) can literally be translated as 'corresponding to' which suggests partnership.

In Genesis 2:21–22, we learn that this partner was created from the rib of the original human. Debates continue over the meaning of the word translated as 'rib'. The word *tsela* may also be translated as 'side', such as the side of a cupboard. Scholars argue the case for using 'side' is far more compelling, as this is how *tsela* is translated in numerous contexts through scripture. If we accept this argument, it puts a whole different spin on the creation story. So, did the gods take one side of the original androgynous human and split it into two?

There are further accounts that support this view. The authors of the book of Genesis were influenced by Babylonian culture, which held the view that early humans were androgynous. The word 'androgyny' originates from the Greek, meaning 'man-woman'. This leads us to another creation myth. In the 5th-century BC Greek philosopher Plato's *Symposium* there were originally three types of human: a man-man, a man-woman, and a woman-woman. All three were much like conjoined twins (back to back) but were split in two later as a punishment. The story was used to explain sexual attraction. The two halves were destined to seek each other out and find completion, that is, to seek their other half or better half. Indeed, we still use such imagery today when we talk about finding our soul mate or being an item. In Genesis 2:24, the two new humans are described as cleaving to each other as if 'they become one flesh'.

It is interesting that the Greek story provides an explanation for heterosexual, gay and lesbian sexuality. If men and women are supposed to be from different planets, why did the gods originally make us partners?

Translating texts from one language to another is not an exact science. Invariably a 'good' translation lies with the skill of the translator(s). Like everyone else, translators view the world through a particular set of filters that colour (or cloud) their view. In truth there is no such thing as a definitive translation, just varying degrees of 'spin'.

PARTNERS IN CRIME?

Gardens have boundaries and the Garden of Eden was no exception. The Hebrew word for garden (*gan*) refers to a garden protected by a fence. At the heart of the Garden of Eden was the tree of the knowledge of good and evil. The first human was told not to eat from the tree or 'he-she' would die. So, Genesis is the account of the birth of creation and also the story of the birth of boundaries and black-and-white thinking. Here we see those interconnected zero-one (binary) categories of inside/outside, good/evil and life/death. In fact, in the very first few verses of Genesis, binary categories and boundaries emerge: light/darkness, day/night, Sun/Moon, water/heavens and water/land. Order and structure were represented as black-and-white categories and hard and fast boundaries. However, it wasn't long before boundaries were transgressed and a new binary category of order/disorder was introduced.

Gods had created a serpent that whispered to the woman to eat from the tree at the centre of Eden. She did and shared the fruit with her husband. This revealed the shame of nakedness to them and they clothed themselves. So the binary of public/private was born. The result of their disobedience was enmity between men and women. Thus, the battle of the sexes began with man gaining dominion over woman. Both were forced to leave the protection of the garden.

We can consider the symbolism in this story. Indeed, the psychologist Carl Jung (1875–1961) suggested that many symbols were common to many cultures and we can see this in the story of the Garden of Eden. The serpent is an ancient symbol of wisdom and to emphasize this it is described as 'more subtle than any other creature'. Alternatively, this could be translated as 'more prudent'. The symbol of health and wisdom is represented by a serpent coiled round a staff, a reference to Aesclepius, the Greek god of heal- ing. However, in modern times, we tend to associate the wand of Hermes with the medical profession. This has two serpents entwined round a staff, topped with a pair of wings. Arguably, the twin serpents indicate duplicity, as Hermes was also the god of commerce and thieves; Apollo described him as a schemer, 'subtle beyond all belief'. In ancient Mesopotamia, of which Babylon was part, the god of healing and magic was Ningizzida, sometimes pictured as a serpent with a human head. The serpent is also associated with reading signs, divination and danger. If we pull these themes and associa- tions together, the main theme emerges as the use or misuse of knowledge.

However, most salient are the references to goddesses. The goddess Asherah, associated with ancient sacred sexual rites, is often depicted with serpents and a tree and there has been much speculation as to whether this is The Tree of Life referred to in Genesis. Hebrew and Canaanite women baked loaves in the shape of Asherah which were blessed and ritually eaten and are arguably the origin of modern-day communion. This may help to explain the obscure reference in Genesis 3:19 (RSV), which states: 'In the sweat of your face you shall eat bread till you return to the ground.'

'Asherah' and derivatives appear frequently in scripture, mostly with negative connotations and often mistranslated as 'groves'. This is a reference to the sacred pillars or trees that represented her. Some scholars argue that the sacred pillars were marked with representations of the menstrual cycle and the female genitals, including the clitoris.

Scholars have also speculated whether the Original Sin was in fact a sexual sin because Adam and Eve understood the meaning of nakedness and clothed themselves shortly after. There has also been much conjecture as to whether Asherah was the partner of the Hebrew god, Yahweh (from where we get Jehovah). There were actually many words used for 'god'. The reasons for retaining the different names of God may have stemmed from the same motivation that caused writers to obscure the presence of the goddess. Using the different names of God may have served to unite differing views so that the many images coalesced.

As well as the origin of the battle of the sexes, we have an account of warring ideologies; in other words the proponents of the one-god universe were engaged in intense propaganda. What we see in Chapter 3 of Genesis is the connection between one-god and man, as opposed to the goddess (and hence many-gods) and woman. Thus, we have a series of interconnecting binaries running through this account, such as:

> Good/evil, god/goddess, one-god/multiple gods, domination/partnership, man/woman and life/death.

It is widely accepted that the goddess Asherah was worshipped, indicating resistance to the one-god view. Chapter 3 of Genesis details the consequences of such resistance. Some scholars argue that the worship of Asherah was linked to egalitarian attitudes to gender and partnership relation-ships rather than those based on domination. Nevertheless, the material discussed in this chapter indicates that partnership preceded domination.

The image of the androgynous or hermaphrodite (dual-sexed) human offers another interesting connection: gods and goddesses often have counterparts in other cultures and Asherah is no exception. She has been linked with Ishtar of the Babylonians or Aphrodite of the Greeks. I have already mentioned Hermes (in the context of the serpent) with whom Aphrodite produced Hermaphroditus, and from where we get the modern-day term hermaphrodite. To complete the circle, the Roman name for Aphrodite was none other than Venus.

Central to the story of Adam and Eve are the consequences of the stealing of the (symbolic) forbidden fruit. This gives a whole new meaning to the phrase 'we are what we eat'. Next, I would like to discuss briefly some myths surrounding gender, relationships and food.

Hunters and gathers: we are what we eat

When I saw a book purporting to be the diet of Adam and Eve, I automatically assumed that it must have been a vegetarian diet. Although the first human hermaphrodite was given permission to eat fruit (except from one tree), there was no permission to eat meat (Genesis 1:28); according to the Bible, Adam and Eve were vegetarian. Ironically, Noah was the first person given permission to eat meat and fish (Genesis 9:3); the man with the responsibility for saving all the animals in the big flood was also the first man to have a barbecue. The animals went in two by two and Noah came out twice the size. So, although Adam and Eve are used as the 'evidence' for heterosexual superiority, they are never used as a model of vegetarianism!

There have been various diets purportedly based on (Stone Age) hunger-gatherer principles, such as the 'caveman diet' and the 'Paleolithic diet', which emphasize organic lean meat and vegetables as part of a 'natural' diet. Of course it never occurs to the writers of these diets to switch the emphasis away from meat and that is, in part, because our attitudes to meat consumption are affected by our misconceptions about our Stone Age ancestors.

We have images of aggressive cavemen with clubs dragging their women around by the hair. Often it is assumed that the men did all the hunting for meat while the women stayed close to home and gathered in a few garnishes. In reality, the food-gathering activity of both females and males constituted a larger proportion of the diet than we popularly imagine. When people are hungry and there is an apple tree close by, they eat the apples. They do not make apple sauce in anticipation of the pork chops (which may or may not arrive) for the barbecue. Admittedly, when we look at cave paintings depicting hunting scenes we can infer that such hunts were highly significant to the people. However, this doesn't mean they painted a cave wall every time they ate. It is more likely that the hunt represented a special occasion, just as we record significant events with photographs. Do you take a photograph every time you have dinner?

Furthermore, we often make the assumption that the nuclear family (mother, father and 2.4 children) transcends cultural and historical boundaries. It doesn't. Hunter-gatherers did not necessarily make the connection between having sex and having offspring. It is not clear whether relationships at this time were monogamous. This is a relatively recent convention. Using mathematical modelling of DNA (Deoxyribonucleic acid), the chemical structure that forms chromosomes, some research indicates that in the Paleolithic era the female population era may have been much greater than the male. This suggests that polygamy may have been common. If this is the case, it suggests there were large groups of co-operative females who were probably capable of providing food for themselves.

While on the subject of DNA modelling, numerous researchers trace our common ancestry back to Africa, specifically to a woman. This should not be surprising given that we have already concluded that the default value of the human race is female. The term used in Genesis 2:23, for a woman is *ishshah*. This, quite literally, means a man (*ish*) with a feminine ending (*shah*). And we know from biology that a man is actually a woman with a masculine ending!

Once again, the ubiquitous filters of androcentrism and biological essentialism, distort our view of the past. Just as biological evidence eventually challenged our view of the interaction between egg and sperm, so archaeological evidence questions the nature of gender relationships in hunter-gatherer societies. Women played a full and equal role in daily life and the evidence suggests that these cultures were founded on co-operation rather than domination. Furthermore, evidence from some arts and funeral rites suggests that some women may have enjoyed a high status in their communities.

The partnership enterprise

In her classic book *The Chalice and the Blade*, human rights scholar Riane Eisler presents two cultural models of human history. One of these models is based on the power of the blade – a hierarchical society based on domination – and many modern-day cultures are still based on this model. The alternative model highlights a society symbolized by the chalice – a culture built on co-operation, consensus and equality. Indeed, our striving for equal opportunities and human rights may be inspired by this view. Of course, these models represent the two extremes of a continuum with varying shades in between.

However, this presents us with yet another genital (chalice/blade) metaphor to consider. Eisler reviews a broad range of evidence throughout history to present a startlingly different picture of our past to the one that is familiar to us. Much of the material she reveals centres on goddess worship and gynocentric (female-centred) cultures and civilizations, thus emphasizing consensus and co-operation. Critics accuse Eisler of presenting an idealized picture of the past that never existed. However, isn't this exactly what happens when we view the world through an androcentric filter? All research evidence is viewed through some type of filter, so different opinions are most often 'filter-clashes' that are based on cultural expectations. Eisler's book is an attempt to awaken us to a possibility that history can be viewed through alternative filters. In contemporary society, there is less diversity in world attitudes, cultures and behaviours and we often interpret this as a natural development or a product of becoming more 'civilized'. However, we should not forget that the European 'discovery' of new worlds also led to the wholesale destruction of alternative cultures and civilizations (viewpoints), including different concepts of gender, community and relationships.

Language has a powerful effect on how we perceive the world and it is easy to fall into the trap of viewing things in black-and-white categories. The words 'androcentric' and 'gynocentric' not only have a particular cultural emphasis but also help support the notion that we are playing the old zero-sum game. Is there no middle ground?

Eisler coins the term 'gylany', which is made up of 'gy' from 'gyno' (woman) and 'an' from 'andro' (man); the 'l' in the middle of the word represents the Greek verb *lyo* or *lyein* meaning 'to solve or resolve' or 'to dissolve or set free'. In negotiating terms we are talking about a 'win-win' situation.

The German word *gestalt* is used in psychology to refer to our perception that 'the whole is greater than the sum of its parts'. Again, we are talking about partnership or teamwork. The success of the 1960s pop group, The Beatles, illustrate perfectly the meaning of *gestalt*. No one could have predicted the results of those four individuals working together: as a group, The Beatles was greater than the sum of its parts. The aspiration is that relationships and societies based on gylany can be too.

In her book *The Power of Partnership, Seven Relationships That Will Change Your Life*, Riane Eisler offers practical applications of the ideas she introduced in *The Chalice and the Blade*. Although we tend to think of relationships as something between people, Eisler first asks us to consider our relationship to ourselves and the impact of gender stereotypes (health and coping styles) on us. This is important, especially if we are living our lives according to rigid roles and expectations. Eisler argues that the self-relationship may have an impact on our intimate relationships and those in the workplace and community. The pattern continues in our national and international relations, including our relationship with nature and the environment. The seventh relationship suggested by Eisler is a spiritual one. Whether or not you believe in a god or goddess (or just a nameless creative force), ultimately this relationship completes the cycle so we can reconsider our relationship with ourselves and our place in the grand scheme of things.

It is easy to dismiss the notion of relationships based on partnership and consensus as something that other people did at another time. However, we often talk about 'partners', so obviously the concept is not totally alien to our modern psyche. Consensus-based, non-hierarchical partnerships do work in the real world. Many gay and lesbian relationships provide us with examples of this, as here there is not necessarily a division of labour based on the roles taken in sexual acts, as gender roles tend to be more flexible and thus such boundaries are blurred.

If we apply the different planet approach to lesbian and gay relationships, we can see the all-pervading gender filters at work. We'd have to assume that the couple would get on perfectly because they were from the same planet. On the other hand, if they both played their roles according to type, they would never have sex. Similarly, some domestic chores would never be done.

There is often an assumption in gay relationships that there have to be male and female roles. With this supposition comes the conclusion that the person who gets 'screwed' physically in the relationship is also the one who gets 'screwed' economically. Following this, the lesbian with the dildo must be the breadwinner. In my own research, when asking who initiates sexual activity, there was an evident tendency for the participants to describe the 'penetrator' as the one that 'does the work'. However, the one who does the work in the bedroom may be the one who 'slaves over a hot stove'. The one who lies back and thinks of the 'Motherland' may well be the one who mows the lawn or does the oil change for the car. There may be no defined roles 'in the bedroom' nor a division of labour, except that based on individual ability.

Inevitably, some lesbian and gay relationships do conform to the traditional, stereotypical, 'different planet' model. The crucial factor is that of mutuality and informed consent. This means that people need to have at least considered their options and other possibilities in terms of their gender roles and the way they relate to one another.

Conclusion: items on the gender agenda

In his book *Body Language,* former salesman turned self-help guru Allan Pease observes that couples in restaurants would much prefer to sit side by side, (a 'co-operative' seating arrangement). However, because restaurants are arranged to maximize floor space, they are 'forced' to sit opposite each other This is a more 'confrontational' arrangement. In other words, couples are inclined towards co-operation but social situations force them into a 'head-on' approach. In many ways, restaurant seating provides a metaphor for what happens in many relationships. We don't necessarily want to take sides, but often feel compelled, through socialization from an early age, to do so by exaggerated gender roles. There is often a clash between what comes naturally and the demands and expectations of social situations.

So what is likely to be in your 'director's cut' of your gender and relationships movie? Is it co-operation or alien-nation? Is it the Great Divide or the great 'coming together'? Are you happy in black and white or do you relish a little more Technicolor? Hopefully, you have at least some food for thought that will allow you to review some of the things we often take for granted.

In this chapter we have questioned the inevitability of a hierarchical view of relationships and considered the proposition that partnership models of relating have precedence over domination. We have explored the idea that human partnership/consensus relationship models preceded those based on domination/hierarchy. At the heart of partnership relationships is the concept of more flexible gender roles. In the next chapter we will consider an alternative model of gender rather than one based on genital shape.

8

Gender Blending: There's More To You Than Pink or Blue

Colour is uncontainable. It effortlessly reveals the limits of language and evades our best attempts to impose a rational order on it... To work with colour is to become acutely aware of the insufficiency of language and theory
— David Batchelor, artist (b.1955)

The world is your kaleidoscope, and the varying combinations of colours which at every succeeding moment it presents to you are the exquisitely adjusted pictures of your ever-moving thoughts — James Allen, artist (1894–1964)

They who know how to appreciate colour relationships, the influence of one colour on another, their contrasts and dissonances, is promised an infinitely diverse imagery
— Sonia Delaunay-Terk, French painter (1885–1979)

PREVIEW

In this chapter we will:

* Consider an alternative personality-based colour-coded gender system.
* Use personality tests to assign a gender colour.
* Consider relationships between different colour-coded genders.

Team colours: A question of sport?

Thinking about it, we often use sporting metaphors when considering the 'game' of love and our perception of sexuality. You have probably heard the expression 'He bats for the other team', as a euphemism for a sexual orientation that is different from – or implicitly opposite to – your own. The idea of belonging to opposing teams is embedded in our psyche, perhaps from the moment we are dressed in our 'team' colours: blue for a boy and pink for a girl. It's not so much a question of playing for the team but living for it. However, whenever people over-identify with their team, it is often at the expense of something else. By over-identifying with one gender role we alienate and make an adversary of half of the human experience.

Watching sporting events, I often wonder why they are still segregated along gender lines. Why aren't events arranged by height or weight differences? One sport that does have different divisions of weight is boxing, which means all the heavyweights fight each other and all the flyweights fight each other. However, in recent years, women have started to compete in the boxing ring, so now a gender division has been added to the weight divisions. But why can't a man and a woman fight each other if they are in the same weight division? For many this is unthinkable. But why? Does our reluctance stem from the need to protect women from the likelihood of physical harm or to protect men from wounded pride?

Undeniably, there is a crossover in terms of ability between women and men. Some women are far more capable of competing in some sporting events than some men. So why not let the capable men and women compete with each other? The truth is that the real issue relates to the traditional (idealized) views of masculinity and femininity: it's about maintaining a crisp and clear division between men and women across all aspects of human experience. Often, such black-and-white distinctions only occur in the world due to social convention.

Of course, when talking about propagating the species, the distinctions are far clearer as penises and vaginas enter into the equation – although with the advent of modern reproductive technologies even this is debatable. For the purpose of making babies we make biological distinctions. However, with regards to sporting events the differences are largely social and cultural. Generally speaking there are two basic sets of genitals (although there can be variations). Is it a leap of logic to say our genitals determine our personalities and our ability to relate to one another? Imagine the outcry should someone even consider applying this faulty logic to suggest that different skin colours originate from different planets.

What would happen if we divided the world into short people and tall people? It makes a lot of sense, especially if we adhere to the flimsy metaphor of 'seeing eye-to-eye'. Physically tall and short people would see eye-to-eye, but does this mean that they must see eye-to-eye in every other way? We've inferred social, cultural and psychological implications from a physical characteristic – is this a ludicrous suggestion? Is it any more absurd to suggest that having an out-going genital shape determines personality or that outwardly shaped genitals equate to outgoing personalities and are therefore a perfect match with inward-looking people with inwardly shaped genitals? Is it possible that a person with 'out-going' genitals might be more introspective or that a person with 'inward-looking' genitals might be a real go-getter? It is possible that a whole spectrum of human experience doesn't necessarily have to spring from the contents of our pink or blue 'team' underwear?

Colour Me Gender

In *The Apartheid of Sex*, human rights scholar Martine Rothblatt proposes a challenge to traditional views of gender roles and relationships. Instead of a scheme based on the shape of human genitals, she offers one based on three colour-coded personality traits, giving a whole spectrum of gender identities. Her original scheme used three primary colour pigments. However, since we have been extensively talking about filters and lenses, it seems logical to re-conceptualize the scheme using the light spectrum.

This fits in with the idea of gender as a performance in social and cultural contexts as gender roles are something we act out rather than something we intrinsically are. Biologically, we are female and male but we *perform* the gender. Lighting is also easier to change. We have discussed how perception filters our experience of the world. Lighting also uses (coloured) filters, which change the mood. The change from pigment colours also helps avoid any (unintentional) confusion or connotation with skin colour. So let's look at the three light sources that we shall call our 'spectrogender'.

Spectrogender uses the same three personality characteristics put forward in Rothblatt's original scheme. The three primary light sources and their associated personality characteristics are:

RED	for	Eroticism
GREEN	for	Nurturing
BLUE	for	Assertiveness

The combination of the three primary colours of light is less predictable (and less familiar) than the colours of a paint box. So, put aside any notions of colour symbolism as this will only cloud the issue. Complete the quiz comprising attitude statements and ratings on personality traits below. You can also take into account your partner's perceptions. Later you will discover a range of ways to code the quiz in order to discover the different and shifting shades of your gender. Hopefully you will find this a little more thought-provoking or enlightening than peering into your underwear.

Spectrogender personality tests

For each of the three components of the spectrogender personality quiz there are 15 attitude statements, followed by five personality traits.

A: Attitude statements

* Rate each attitude statements using a scale of 0 to 10. Zero means you totally disagree and 10 means you totally agree.
* The numbers in between represent various shades of agreement/ disagreement. So, take 5 as a mid-point, meaning neutral, that is you neither agree nor disagree.
* Use any whole numbers in the range.

B: Personality traits

* For each of the five personality traits rate yourself on a scale of 0 to 10. Then rate them from the perspective of a partner or ask your partner to complete this part themselves.
* If you don't have a current partner you can complete the quiz from the perspective of your last partner. Alternatively, just leave this section blank; the scoring of the quiz allows for this possibility: you simply double your own score.
* Simply read the statement through, don't agonize over it too much; often your gut reaction is best.
* Give each statement a rating from 0 to 10 that most closely reflects your attitude. You should only use the whole numbers. No fractions please.

Sex, Lies and Stereotypes

1. BLUE SCORE (ASSERTIVE)
A: ATTITUDE STATEMENTS

Rate each attitude statement using any number in the scale of 0 to 10.

> 0 = totally disagree
> 5 = neutral
> 10 = totally agree

1. _____ I say no without apology if people make unreasonable demands on me.
2. _____ I am able to express directly my discontent to a friend/partner if I think it's justified.
3. _____ I express my opinions, even if others in the group disagree with me.
4. _____ If people sitting nearby kept talking in the cinema, I would ask them to be quiet.
5. _____ I find it easy to ask friends for small favours.
6. _____ I would speak to my neighbours if they were too noisy.
7. _____ I prefer to 'nip problems in the bud'.
8. _____ When I think a person is being unfair I draw his/her attention to it.
9. _____ I am rarely reluctant to communicate my thoughts and feelings.
10. _____ I do **not** avoid dealing with confrontational situations.
11. _____ I often feel intimidated by opinionated people.
12. _____ It is difficult for me to refuse a door-to-door salesperson when they are nice.
13. _____ I often end up saying 'yes' when I really wanted to say 'no'.
14. _____ I sometimes show my anger by swearing at or belittling another person.
15. _____ I often sulk to make my point or to get my own way.

B: PERSONALITY TRAITS

How would you rate yourself on the following traits using the 0 to 10 scale?

> 0 = not at all
> 10 = totally

| _____ Assertive | _____ Self-assured | _____ Decisive |
| _____ Direct | _____ Confident | _____ **Total** |

How would your partner rate you on the same traits using the 0 to 10 scale?

_____ Assertive _____ Self-assured _____ Decisive

_____ Direct _____ Confident _____ **Total**

Scoring

* Add together scores for items numbered 1 to 10.
  This is **Score A** _____
* Add together scores for items numbered 11 to 15.
  This is **Score B** _____
* Now do this sum: 25 minus (-) **Score B** = **Score C** _____
* Add together ALL the scores for the traits (of both you and your partner).
  This is **Score D** _____
* If you left the partner score blank, simply double **Score D**.
* Now add together all the scores: **Score A** + **Score C** + **Score D**.
  This is your **ASSERTIVENESS SCORE** _____
* **Bonus points:** Give yourself up to 5 points if you DON'T get off on being aggressive _____
* This score should be between 0 and 255. If it isn't you need to go back and check your calculations.

NEW ASSERTIVENESS TOTAL SCORE _____

2. GREEN SCORE (NURTURING)

A: ATTITUDE STATEMENTS

Rate each attitude statement using any number in the scale of 0 to 10.

0 = totally disagree
10 = totally agree
5 = neutral

1. _____ I support other people emotionally.
2. _____ I can easily put myself in another person's shoes.
3. _____ It is relatively easy for me to express positive emotions toward another person.

4. _____ I express my attachment to someone with tender words and gentle considerations.
5. _____ People tend to come to me with their problems.
6. _____ I'm told I'm a good listener.
7. _____ I am sensitive to the needs of others.
8. _____ I would not feel ashamed to cry in front of my friends.
9. _____ I am quick to spot when someone in a group is feeling awkward or uncomfortable.
10. _____ I often become emotionally involved in sad movies.
11. _____ Seeing people cry doesn't really upset me.
12. _____ I often feel people take advantage of my good nature.
13. _____ People often say I'm emotionally cold or distant.
14. _____ Talking about feelings is just self-indulgent.
15. _____ I always put the needs of others before my own.

B: PERSONALITY TRAITS

How would you rate yourself on the following traits using the 0 to 10 scale?

0 = not at all
10 = totally

| _____ Nurturing | _____ Compassionate | _____ Sensitive |
| _____ Tender | _____ Caring | _____ **Total** |

How would your partner rate you on the same traits using the 0 to 10 scale?

| _____ Nurturing | _____ Compassionate | _____ Sensitive |
| _____ Tender | _____ Caring | _____ **Total** |

Scoring

* Add together scores for items numbered 1 to 10.
  This is **Score A** _____
* Add together scores for items numbered 11 to 15.
  This is **Score B** _____
* Now do the sum: 25 minus (-) **Score B** = **Score C** _____
* Add together ALL the scores for the traits (of both you and your partner).

This is **Score D** _____

* If you left the partner score blank, simply double **Score D**.
* Now add all the scores together: **Score A + Score C + Score D**.
   This is your **NURTURE SCORE** _____
* Bonus points: Give yourself up to 5 points if you DON'T enjoy being self-sacrificing _____
* This score should be between 0 and 255. If it isn't you need to go back and check your calculations.
   NEW NURTURE TOTAL SCORE _____

3. RED SCORE (EROTICISM)

A: ATTITUDE STATEMENTS

Rate each attitude statement using any number in the scale of 0 to 10.

> 0 = totally disagree
> 10 = totally agree
> 5 = neutral

1. _____ I know my body well and know what pleases me sexually.
2. _____ I truly express myself sexually.
3. _____ I feel good about myself after sex.
4. _____ I would feel comfortable talking about my sexual desires with my partner.
5. _____ There's more to sex than genitals.
6. _____ I feel comfortable initiating sex.
7. _____ I am sexually adventurous.
8. _____ I would feel comfortable letting my partner watch me masturbate.
9. _____ I take responsibility for my sexual health.
10. _____ I have had fantasies about sex with someone of the same gender as me.
11. _____ People shouldn't have to work at having a good sex life, it should just happen.
12. _____ Real sex begins when penetrative intercourse begins.
13. _____ The thought of two people of the same gender (two men/two women) having sex repulses me.

14. _____ I would never consider letting anyone sexually stimulate my anus.
15. _____ Sex doesn't play a very important part in my life.

B: PERSONALITY TRAITS

How would you rate yourself on the following traits using the 0 to 10 scale?

    0 = not at all
    10 = totally

| _____ Erotic | _____ Sexy | _____ Passionate |
| _____ Hot | _____ Up-for-it | _____ **Total** |

How would your partner rate you on the same traits using the 0 to 10 scale?

| _____ Erotic | _____ Sexy | _____ Passionate |
| _____ Hot | _____ Up-for-it | _____ **Total** |

Scoring

* Add together scores for items numbered 1 to 10.
  This is **Score A** _____
* Add together scores for items numbered 11 to 15.
  This is **Score B** _____
* Now do the sum: 25 minus (-) **Score B** = **Score C** _____
* Add together ALL the scores for the traits (of both you and your partner).
  This is **Score D** _____
* If you left the partner score blank, simply double **Score D**.
* Now add together **Score A** + **Score C** + **Score D**.
  This is your **EROTICISM SCORE** _____
* Bonus points: Give yourself up to 5 points if you feel extra-sexy today!
* This score should be between 0 and 255. If it isn't you need to go back and check your calculations.
  NEW EROTICISM TOTAL SCORE _____

For the purposes of this chapter we need to collapse each of the scores into one of three categories:

Low = 0 to 99
Moderate = 100 to 199
High = 200 to 255

BLUE _____   GREEN _____   RED _____

If you find that your scores are close to the boundaries, you may want to consider looking at both categories. For instance, if you score 101 or 99, you could look at the LOW and MODERATE. In this case you need to go with your own feelings about which is the most appropriate category for you. You may choose both. It's up to you.

Before we consider other methods of coding the quiz, let's look at what spectral shade your basic scores produced.

SPECTROGENDER COLOUR CHART

Simply find your combination/s or scores in the table opposite to find your spectrogender. The order of presentation of shades in the table has no significance. They are presented merely for convenience.

So what does it all mean? Well on one level it is every bit as arbitrary as gender based on genital shape. However, with spectrogender there is a whole spectrum of gender based on personality traits. So, what evolves is a visual representation of our gender.

If someone achieves three high scores on all three personality traits, then expect a fanfare of the five tones. We have 'Close Encounters of the Gendered Kind' in a halo of pure white light! As a general rule, the paler the tone of light the greater the androgyny. White light represents some-one who is highly androgynous and highly erotic. At the opposite end of the spectrum, three low scores indicate someone who is undifferentiated, and, possibly, also asexual (little interest in sexual matters).

There are various shades of androgyny. Pale Turquoise represents androgyny with moderate eroticism. Cyan (peacock blue) represents androgyny with low eroticism. Red indicates undifferentiated gender with high eroticism. Brown represents undifferentiated gender with moderate eroticism. Both red and brown indicate someone for whom sex has a high

RED (Eroticism)	GREEN (Nurture)	BLUE (Assertiveness)	SPECTROGENDER
High	High	High	**WHITE LIGHT** (androgynous)
High	High	Moderate	**LEMON**
High	High	Low	**YELLOW**
High	Moderate	High	**PALE PINK**
High	Moderate	Moderate	**PEACH**
High	Moderate	Low	**ORANGE**
High	Low	High	**MAGENTA**
High	Low	Moderate	**CERISE**
High	Low	Low	**RED (PRIMARY)** (undifferentiated)
Moderate	High	High	**PALE TURQUOISE** (androgynous)
Moderate	High	Moderate	**PASTEL GREEN**
Moderate	High	Low	**LIME GREEN**
Moderate	Moderate	High	**LILAC**
Moderate	Moderate	Moderate	**GREY (SHADOW)**
Moderate	Moderate	Low	**OLIVE GREEN**
Moderate	Low	High	**PURPLE**
Moderate	Low	Moderate	**VIOLET**
Moderate	Low	Low	**BROWN**
Low	High	High	**CYAN (BLUE)** (androgynous)
Low	High	Moderate	**LIGHT GREEN**
Low	High	Low	**GREEN (PRIMARY)**
Low	Moderate	High	**LIGHT BLUE**
Low	Moderate	Moderate	**TEAL (BLUE)**
Low	Moderate	Low	**DARK GREEN**
Low	Low	High	**BLUE (PRIMARY)**
Low	Low	Moderate	**INDIGO**
Low	Low	Low	**DARKNESS** (undifferentiated)

degree of importance in their lives. However, they may indicate a lack of efficacy in the real world and possible emotional detachment.

Here is a summary of the spectrogender for which there are low scores on the three personality dimensions:

Lower levels of assertiveness

Yellow, orange, red (primary), lime green, olive green, brown, green (primary), dark green and darkness.

Lower levels of nurture

Magenta, cerise, red (primary), purple, violent, brown, green (primary), dark green and darkness.

Lower levels of eroticism

Cyan, light green, green (primary), light blue, teal, dark green, blue (primary), indigo and darkness.

At this stage you may want to go back and complete the whole exercise again, but this time answering all of the questions according to your *ideal*. How would you ideally like to respond? This will give you a colour-coded ideal spectrogender. It is then possible to incorporate these colours into the visualization technique explored in the next chapter.

Alternatively, you may decide to work on one of your low scores. I suggest that you focus on your blue (assertiveness) and green (nurturance) scores first of all. These represent the concepts of instrumentality (blue) and expressiveness (green) discussed in chapter 6 on health. High scores for both of these traits approximate to the concept of androgyny.

To boost your scores, go back to your responses and see where your low scores occur. If your score is low for assertiveness, you may consider getting a self-help book on assertiveness and practising the exercises. There is a strong degree of crossover between assertiveness and confidence. We often mistakenly assume that confidence is something people have rather than something people do. However, it is often not realized that the more confidently people behave the easier it becomes for them to feel confident. So, by assuming an attitude of confidence and doing the kind of things confident and assertive people do, you can 'gain' confidence. Similarly, if you have a low score for nurture, you first need to go back and review your low scores. You may want to consider taking a short course to learn basic counselling skills, which may help you to listen and empathize.

Specific emotions or feelings do not belong to one gender or another, they are human qualities: we learn to emphasize some qualities and suppress others. However, we can choose to change the emphasis. For example, if your spectrogender is yellow, you will have a high eroticism score and a high nurture score, but a low assertiveness score. If that works for you, that's fine, but occasionally you may find yourself saying 'yes' when you really mean 'no'. After taking the Spectrogender Personality quiz again for your ideal, your outcome may be lemon. To achieve lemon in reality, you will need to work on your assertiveness. You can do this by reading self-help books, taking a short course or simply by starting to assume the attitude (and behaviour) of an assertive person. This isn't about changing the real you, it's about asserting the real you.

We will consider some self-help techniques in the next chapter. Meanwhile, let's look at the possible colour combinations of genders in relationships.

Spectral relationships: somewhere over the rainbow

We seem to hold two opposing views about which types of relationships work. On one hand we maintain that 'opposites attract' and, on the other, we say that 'birds of a feather flock together'. The research evidence most strongly indicates that similarity forms the strongest foundation for a relationship. Often we focus on superficial qualities that create the illusion of two very different people. However, beneath the surface, the people in the relationship share similar beliefs, attitudes and values. So let's consider the matching or clashing of our spectrogender.

There are three basic rules to consider when deciding whether spectrogenders go together:

Similar

Colours similar to one another will go together because they share roughly the same distributions of the three primary colours (such as orange and yellow or shades of blue and green). For instance, a cyan spectrogender comprises low eroticism, high nurture and high assertiveness. A light green spectrogender comprises low eroticism, high nurture and moderate assertiveness. There is a high degree of similarity.

Tonal

Colours that are variations on the same colour work well together, such as yellow and lemon, or orange and peach. For instance, a yellow spectrogender comprises high eroticism, high nurture and low assertiveness. A lemon spectrogender comprises high eroticism, high nurture and moderate assertiveness. Thus, there is a strong basis for agreement.

Complementary

Sometimes colours that provide the greatest degree of contrast may be considered complementary because they 'balance each other out'. However, such combinations are also most likely to clash. Most of these combinations are variations on the 'different planet' approach. Let's consider the magenta/green combination. Magenta includes high eroticism, low nurture and high assertiveness; while green includes low eroticism, high nurture and low assertiveness. Thus, on all three traits they are opposites and the potential for a clash is much greater.

It is important to recognize that these spectral shades of gender are approximations, merely snapshots. We've already discussed in chapter 3 how personality traits are highly susceptible to situational changes. After all, you wouldn't judge a movie by one frame, would you? So, let's look at the table of combinations on pages 142–3. By and large, for the final column assume that traits are opposites (high-to-low) unless otherwise stated.

All these shades represent approximations. The scores have been broken down into three broad categories. Clashes are only likely to occur when the scores are at the extreme ends of the scales (high versus low). Going back to your original scores for the traits will indicate the extent of the difference.

Spectrogender is about highlighting patterns of interactive style, in some ways an aim shared with the 'different planet' approach. However, spectrogender is *not* about essential differences. In contrast to the 'different planet' approach, if people in a relationship choose to change, it is not about changing to a prescribed ideal based on your genital 'birthright', it is about both people becoming more rounded human beings.

You might want to think of the spectrogender as your gender aura. The gender roles we play reflect various combinations of light. Thus, two people may have the same spectrogender but have a different type of genitals. People with the same type of genitals may have very different coloured spectrogenders. Let's consider the implications in greater detail.

The path to gender enlightenment

In chapter 3 we considered the concept of androgyny, a term used to describe someone who displays high levels of both masculinity and femininity. In chapter 6 we described the traits usually associated with masculinity as *instrumental* traits; instrumentality is about acting in a task-oriented or goal-directed way. For traits usually associated with femininity we used the term *expressive* traits; expressiveness is about displaying emotion and empathy, acting in an emotion-focused or relationship-focused way. Thus, the terms instrumental and expressive remove some of the emphasis on traditional gender-role stereotypes. Spectrogender takes this one step further: terms such as androgyny, expressiveness and instrumentality are abstract concepts and difficult to picture. Simple colour coding helps to overcome this barrier and provides something more tangible. It also removes the emphasis from biological essentialism, in that spectrogender does not discriminate on the basis of biology or sexuality.

The concepts of nurture (green) and assertiveness (blue) approximate to the concepts of expressiveness and instrumentality respectively. Not surprisingly then, high levels of both nurturance and assertiveness approximate to the concept of androgyny. Another word for androgyny is 'balanced', that is, living the whole of the human experience not just half of it. We can link this to the exercise on 'comfort' on page 102. Higher androgyny is associated with being comfortable in a range of situations that require a range of different behaviours, traits and emotions. It's about greater choice. Even if spectrogender is just a bit of fun, then at least it's a bit of fun where you have the last laugh.

Conclusion: Life is a many gendered thing

Spectrogender is not meant be a definitive guide for relationships nor does it offer quick-fix solutions. It looks at personalities rather than anatomy

SPECTROGENDER	SIMILAR	TONAL	COMPLEMENT/ CLASH
LEMON (Dominant traits: eroticism and nurture)	Other pastel tones, particularly green and peach	Shades of yellow and lime green	**INDIGO** Assertiveness balanced
YELLOW (Dominant traits: eroticism and nurture)	Orange and green	Shades of yellow and lime green	**BLUE** **(PRIMARY)**
PALE PINK (Dominant traits: eroticism and assertiveness)	Red	Shades of pink	**DARK GREEN**
PEACH (Dominant traits: eroticism. Balanced: nurture and assertiveness)	Other pastel shades, particularly pink and lemon	Shades of orange	**TEAL** Nurture balanced Assertiveness balanced
ORANGE (Dominant traits: Eroticism)	Red and yellow	Peach and shades of orange	**LIGHT BLUE** Nurture balanced
MAGENTA (Dominant traits: eroticism and assertiveness)	Red and purple	Red and shades of pink	**GREEN** **(PRIMARY)**
CERISE (Dominant traits: eroticism)	Red and purple	Red and shades of pink	**LIGHT GREEN** Assertiveness balanced
RED (PRIMARY) (Dominant trait: eroticism)	Purple, pink and orange	Shades of pink	**CYAN**
PALE TURQUOISE (Dominant traits: nurture and assertiveness)	Other pastel shades particularly green and blue	Cyan and teal	**BROWN** Eroticism balanced
PASTEL GREEN (Dominant trait: nurture)	Other pastel shades particularly yellow and blue	Shades of green	**VIOLET** Eroticism balanced Assertiveness balanced
LIME GREEN (Dominant trait: nurture)	Yellow and green	Shades of green and yellow	**PURPLE** Eroticism balanced
LILAC (Dominant traits: assertiveness)	Other pastel shades particularly pink and blue	Shades of purple	**OLIVE GREEN** Eroticism balanced Nurture balanced
MID-GREY (SHADOW) (No dominant traits: all three balanced)	Grey and other mid-tones.	Shades of grey, earth tones (olive green, brown)	**MID-GREY** **(SHADOW)** All three balanced

SPECTROGENDER	SIMILAR	TONAL	COMPLEMENT/ CLASH
OLIVE GREEN (Dominant traits: nurture)	Yellow, green and blue	Shades of green	**LILAC** Eroticism balanced Nurture balanced
PURPLE (Dominant traits: assertiveness)	Blue and dark pink and indigo	Shades of purple	**LIME GREEN** Eroticism balanced
VIOLET	Blue and dark pink	Shades of purple and indigo	**PASTEL GREEN** Eroticism balanced Assertiveness balanced
BROWN	Orange and red	Shades of orange	**PALE TURQUOISE** Eroticism balanced
CYAN (BLUE) (Dominant traits: nurture and assertiveness)	Blue and green	Shades of turquoise and teal	**RED (PRIMARY)**
LIGHT GREEN (Dominant traits: nurture)	Yellow and blue	Shades of blue	**CERISE** Assertiveness balanced
GREEN (Dominant traits: nurture)	Yellow and blue	Shades of green	**MAGENTA**
LIGHT BLUE (Dominant traits: assertiveness)	Mid-green and purple	Shades of blue	**ORANGE** Nurture balanced Assertiveness balanced
TEAL (BLUE)	Green and blue	Cyan and turquoise shades	**PEACH** Nurture balanced Assertiveness balanced
DARK GREEN	Yellow and blue	Shades of green	**PALE PINK** Nurture balanced
BLUE (PRIMARY) (Dominant traits: assertiveness)	Green and purple	Shades of blue	**YELLOW**
INDIGO	Blue and purple	Shades of blue and purple	**LEMON** Assertiveness balanced
WHITE LIGHT (Dominant traits: eroticism, nurture and assertiveness)	Other lighter tones (i.e. lemon, pale turquoise and pink)	Other lighter tones (i.e. lemon, pale turquoise and pink)	**DARKNESS/ DARKER TONES** Total imbalance
DARKNESS (Dominant traits: none)	Other dark tones (such as indigo, brown and dark green)	Other darker tones (such as indigo, brown and dark green)	**WHITE LIGHT/ LIGHTER TONES** Total imbalance

and therefore can be used for any sexual relationship between consenting adults. It offers 27 possible genders with numerous possible relationship combinations. The point is that the whole spectrogender scheme should be used as a starting point for discussion, not as the goal. If your relationship does not fit in into the spectrogender scheme, but works anyway, then that's fine, after all 'if it ain't broke don't fix it'. Thinking and talking about personal development issues is what's important, not whether you come to the same conclusions as everyone else.

So, what is a normal relationship? In the past 'normal' has simply been a case of 'what you are used to', now, increasingly, it's a case of 'what you choose'. In the next chapter we will consider some personal development techniques to help reframe relationships in a more positive light.

Changing Views: What You See Is What You Get!

Even comparatively simple acts of perception are very much more at the mercy of the social patterns... than we might suppose – Edward Sapir, anthropologist (1884–1939)

The world is presented in a kaleidoscopic flux of impressions which have to be organized by our minds... We cut nature up and organize it into concepts, and ascribe significance... All observers are not led by the same physical evidence to the same picture of the universe – Benjamin Whorf, anthropologist (1897–1941)

No one sees the world with pristine eyes – Ruth Benedict, anthropologist (1887–1948)

PREVIEW

In this chapter we will:

* Review the psychological literature to show that often we see what we expect to see.
* Look at some exercises to help 'reframe' gender roles and human relationships in a different light.
* Consider some suggestions to improve communication skills and negotiating styles.

WYSIWYG

WYSIWYG (pronounced 'wizzy-wig') is a computer acronym meaning: *What You See Is What You Get.* Basically it means that what you see on the screen is what you will get when you print it out. I've already suggested that our cultural norms are rather like a computer operating system, so let's develop this idea further.

Our operating system includes basic human processing abilities. Have you ever used a word-processor package where the automatic features kick in? Faster than a speeding bullet point: where there's one, too many more are sure to follow. Automatic features and predictive text work on the basis of pattern seeking, probability and expectation.

It is rather like the filters we have been talking about throughout this book. In chapter 2 we discussed the function of attitudes. The word 'attitude' means 'fit and reaction for action'. The example used was one of an athlete primed and ready to go. As human information processors, we are primed to respond in predictable ways. This phenomenon is known as 'perceptual set' or 'personal perceptual filters' so essentially: What You Perceive Is What You See Is What You Get. However, I think the acronym WYPIWYSIWYG (wippy-wizzy-wig) is a little too much!

Perceptual perceptual filters work to focus our attention on certain aspects of information, which are based on prior expectations. In many ways we perceive what we think we ought to perceive, based on what we have typically perceived in the past. Our expectations are shaped by cultural and personal experiences, so sometimes we wrongly perceive things we have not seen before. That is, we distort our perceptions to fit our expectations. The truth is that, in many ways, we perceive what we want to perceive. An underlying theme is the drive for continuity in our perceptions and often we are not even aware that personal perceptual filters are at work.

However, if our personal perceptual filters are largely learned we can discover how to use them to our advantage too. Let me give you an example of how amenable our personal perceptual filters are to change. Imagine you buy a new car and it's red. The first day you drive the car you suddenly notice how many other red cars there are on the road. What has happened is that your personal perceptual filter has changed. A red car has now become important in your life and as a result your personal perceptual filter has changed to reflect this.

It's WYSIWYG in reverse, so that's WYGIWYS (wiggy-wizz): What You've Got Is What You See.

KEEP YOUR EYES ON THE ROAD

Motorists who take the advanced driving test are taught to look where they want to go, rather than at the obstacles they want to avoid. The reasoning for this is that we are drawn to what we focus on. Concentrating on obstacles means you will drive into them. Have you ever wondered why mountaineers don't look down? The answer is simple; they don't want to go down, they want to go up, so that's where they look. All too often we are inspired by dreams, goals and ambitions, but spend far too much time fixating on life's obstacles so we fail to see where we are going. To succeed, we need to tune into what we want rather than what we want to avoid.

It's good to glance in the rear-view mirror, but not at the expense of looking where we are going. It's good to know where we came from, but it's also essential to keep our eyes on the road ahead. If we are going to resolve our problems we need to look forward.

If we consider the 'different planet' approach to gender and relationships we see the exact reverse at work. If problems in relationships are even partly due to rigid gender roles, then does it make sense to portray those roles as being even more rigid than they already are? The fact that we believe that men and women act as though they are from different planets merely sets up this expectation in our personal perceptual filters. Not surprisingly, we amass the evidence as easily as we count the red cars the day after we've purchased one. What you see is what you get. If you see men and women as being from different planets, you will find the evidence to support your view. It won't help you one bit in finding a solution to rigid gender roles other than to stay in the same mind-set that caused the problem. If you were trapped in a maze, would you try to get out by planting more hedges? To find the solution you have to be creative and think outside the square.

THINKING OUTSIDE THE SQUARE

Many of us believe that creativity is a quality that only creative people possess. At the same time, on seeing a modern art installation, many people protest: 'I could have done that!'. The chances are that you probably could and the only reason you didn't was that you didn't think of doing it first. We have discussed throughout this book how boundaries are rarely fixed, and are almost certainly fuzzy. It is only in the illusory shadow-world of black-and-white thinking that people possess all of a trait or none of it. The absolutely yes/no exercise in chapter 3 demonstrated that it is difficult to force our personalities into all-or-nothing categories. You may not be the most creative person in the world ever, but can you honestly say that you have zero creativity? I'm not talking about artistic skill, but about imagination. Are you an imaginative person? Don't answer that question before you have had a look at the brief quiz on imagination on the opposite page. But first, try this simple exercise:

* DO NOT think of a dog.
* That's right DO NOT think of a dog.

Okay, so what kind of dog was it? _____
What colour was it? _____

IMAGINATION QUIZ

For the purposes of the quiz opposite, let's turn black-and-white thinking on its head. You still have only two options for your answers, however this time I'd like you to answer ABSOLUTELY NO or YES. Even if you can only give a one per cent YES, it's still a YES. Please complete the quiz now.

SCORING

* For every YES score 10 points
* For every ABSOLUTELY NO score 0 points
* Give yourself 100 bonus points if you skipped question 13.

If you scored 10 points or more, you are imaginative. There is an element of imagination in most human information processing. If you read a book, you create mental images from the words. Music often transports us to another time or place and may evoke emotions. Watching a TV cookery demonstration can cause us to salivate. Being worried, frightened or superstitious involves an element of imagination as we construct a possible outcome for an event. We often fear the unknown or worry about imaginary consequences. We all dream, whether we remember or not, and they have a strong imaginative component. People may get sexually aroused from words, thoughts or images. If you've ever wondered what it would be like to change biological sex for the day, that also requires imagination. Possibly you

IMAGINATION QUIZ

	A	B
1. Have you ever watched a cookery programme on TV and found your mouth was watering just watching the food being prepared?	ABSOLUTELY YES	NO
2. Have you ever read a book and formed an image of one of the characters in your mind?	ABSOLUTELY YES	NO
3. Have you ever listened to music that evoked emotions or mental images of places or people?	ABSOLUTELY YES	NO
4. Have you ever been worried about something?	ABSOLUTELY YES	NO
5. Have you ever been frightened of something?	ABSOLUTELY YES	NO
6. Have you ever had a dream, a nightmare or a daydream?	ABSOLUTELY YES	NO
7. Have you ever wondered whether there is life on Mars and what it might look like?	ABSOLUTELY YES	NO
8. Have you ever had sexually arousing thoughts or sexual fantasies?	ABSOLUTELY YES	NO
9. Have you ever wondered what it would be like to change biological sex for the day?	ABSOLUTELY YES	NO
10. If you became a multimillionaire can you imagine what you would do with the money?	ABSOLUTELY YES	NO
13. Do you have any superstitions?	ABSOLUTELY YES	NO

couldn't help thinking of a gyrating hair-piece when you read WYSIWYG.

You may have now realized that there is a strong connection between mind and body and between reality and imagination. Mere thoughts can bring about physical changes, such as fear, arousal or salivation. Often the mind and body cannot differentiate between reality and imagination. We can actually use this human quality of the inability to distinguish to our advantage. By strategically using the creative power of our imagination we create changes in the way we view the world. This in turn affects how we live our lives. In fact, the process may have started without you even realizing it. Our personal perceptual filters are highly susceptible to change. You will recall that the example of the red car requires very little effort. The first step to any change is simply creating a mental picture of it. And remember, the way we perceive something affects the way we experience it.

Just from considering the material in this book your personal perceptual filter may have changed slightly. As a theory-driven pattern-seeking human being, now you may be more likely to tune into evidence to support the partnership model of human relationships over the different planet approach. It is also possible to choose to take this process a step further.

Creative visualization

Creative visualization is a technique for using images strategically to change attitudes and perceptions. Top athletes use creative visualization to help improve their performance. We are told that practice makes perfect and on account of the intimate mind/body connection we enjoy, our brains do not distinguish between 'real' practice and that which only takes place in our imagination. So, athletes who rehearse techniques in their imagination actually enjoy measurable improvements in their actual performance. Mental rehearsal helps build pathways in the brain, just like when we do things for real.

Creative visualization techniques are not difficult to learn, mainly because they are simply a refinement of routine human information processing. Anyone can apply the principles to any area of their lives, from improving relationships to developing and improving skills. When we are frightened of something, often we keep rehearsing those fears over and over in our head, which makes us become even more scared. Continuous thinking about a subject increases our physiological arousal, which in turn exacerbates the fear and so the vicious circle continues. On the other hand, we also talk about 'psyching' ourselves up; this is another way of describing creative visualization. The first step is to create a compelling image of what you want.

Before we consider a basic technique for doing this, I want to discuss another aspect of human psychology that you have probably experienced. Often we seem to solve problems spontaneously when we have consciously

Sex, Lies and Stereotypes

stopped trying to do so. However, although our conscious mind is not working on the problem, our subconscious (also called the unconscious) mind continues to do so. Invariably, the solution pops into our heads in a flash of insight. Creative visualization works by helping this natural process along. We set up the ideal scenario and focus on where we want to go and our subconscious mind gets to work on it and fills in the details.

Before considering the process of creative visualization, we need to practise a basic relaxation technique. Relaxation affects your brain waves and so enhances the effects of creative visualization.

Basic relaxation

Pick a time and a place when you are not likely to be disturbed.

* Get into a comfortable position, either sitting or lying.
* Close your eyes and begin breathing deeply and slowly.
* Breathe in to the mental count of four, filling your lungs and feeling your belly expand.
* Hold for a second before breathing out to the mental count of 10, letting your belly contract.
* Repeat the deep breathing three or four times.
* Starting from the tips of your toes and working to the top of your head (crown), let your body relax completely.
* Focus on each part of your body, letting go of any tension and allow the muscles to relax.
* As soon as you reach the top of your crown, begin counting off 10 deep breaths. Each time you exhale say the word 'deeper' as part of the exhaling breath.

You are now in the right state to begin visualizing your image. If you haven't used relaxation techniques before, you may wish to practise this a few times.

The five key components of effective creative visualization are:

1. **Setting** a goal.
2. **Relaxing.**
3. **Creating** a picture.
4. **Focusing** on the picture often.
5. **Charging** the picture with positive mental attitude.

Let's see how we can use creative visualization in conjunction with spectrogender by using the three basic light sources of red, green and blue. Red is associated with eroticism, green with nurturance and blue with assertiveness. Imagine that you want to become more assertive, which means you need more blue light.

1. Setting a Goal

To set a goal simply means to decide on something you would like to happen. In your case your goal is to achieve more assertiveness symbolized by blue light.

* Write down your overall goal; this is the big picture – essentially you want to boost your assertiveness.
* Now write down all of your reasons for wanting to boost your assertiveness.
* Next break the goal down into smaller sub-goals. Think of all the behaviours you associate with being assertive. You may want to review the items in the Spectrogender Personality quiz or think of some of your own. Write these down, too, as research has shown that people who put their goals down on paper are more likely to achieve them.

2. Relaxing

Use the relaxation technique on the previous page to put yourself in the right state to create the mental image.

3. Creating a picture

For the present example, this part is straightforward. Blue light symbolizes greater assertiveness. However, there are a number of ways you could visualize this.

* Imagine your toes beginning to glow with a beautiful blue light which creeps up your body until you glow from head to foot.
* Imagine your spine is a bright blue neon tube that radiates light throughout your whole body.
* Imagine a big blue light above your body that bathes your body in cobalt blue.

However you visualize the blue light is up to you, as long as it's a positive experience. Make it special. As you bathe in the blue light, try to summon up the emotions that go with being more assertive. Feel the energy from the blue light. Don't worry that you have not taken any practical steps at this stage; your subconscious mind will help you fill in the details.

4. Focusing on the picture often

By bringing the mental picture to mind during quiet times of meditation or while daydreaming throughout the day, it begins to become an integral part of your life. Always practise your visualization when you are not likely to be disturbed. If however, you need a quick booster during the day, just close your eyes, take a few deep breaths and imagine being bathed in the blue light.

5. Charging the picture with positive mental attitude

In many ways, with creative visualization, what you put in is what you get out. You can boost the effects by 'suspending your disbelief' and really emerging yourself in the process. It's not difficult. At the very least it's incredibly relaxing. So, rather than saying to yourself: 'Let's see if it works', say 'Let's see how well it works'. The more you try to get into it, the more effective creative visualization will be for you.

So that's basically it. Practised regularly, your desired goals will slowly take form as you recondition your thinking towards success. In mountaineering terms, you are focusing on the peak and not the distance to the ground. The great thing about creative visualization is that it's fun and risk-free. As already mentioned, top athletes who spend time rehearsing in their imagination find real life gains in their performance; creative visualization gives them that all-important edge. The evidence is unequivocal; it really does work. Remember WYSIWYG. Furthermore, supporting your visualization with affirmations, reinforces and enhances its effects.

Affirmations

An affirmation is a positively worded statement of intent. It's a mission statement. You can use an affirmation rather than an image in stage three above (Creating a picture) or combine a picture and an affirmation to increase the efficacy. We routinely engage in mental dialogue with ourselves, which acts as a running commentary to our lives. We can exploit this process by repeating positive self-affirming statements. There are a few basic ground rules:

* Statements should be positively phrased. So instead of 'I will eat less junk food', try 'I will eat more healthily'. Replace a negative (or a double negative) with a positive as we process simple, positive statements more easily.
* Statements should be in the immediate future. If you say, 'I am assertive', this is clearly not true else you wouldn't be trying to be more assertive. However, if you phrase the affirmation as if it is about to happen in incremental steps, it becomes more believable. For instance: 'Increasingly, as each day passes, I am becoming more assertive.' It's more difficult to disagree with this statement. Hence, it has more impact.

If you need a quick boost, take a few deep breaths, close your eyes and mentally repeat your affirmation a few times: 'Increasingly, as each day passes, I am becoming more assertive'.

ADAPTING THE PROCESS FOR MORE SPECIFIC GOALS

Creative visualization can also be used for more specific goals. Break your overall goal down into a number of sub-goals and work on each one in turn. For instance, if one of your sub-goals of being assertive is asking a friend or relative for a small favour, when you create your visualization imagine yourself just having completed the goal. Summon up the emotions that go with the success. Your subconscious mind will fill in the rest.

The basic principles of creative visualization can also be used as a relaxation technique. You will be surprised how different you feel after practising for a few weeks.

The techniques have been presented here as a way of actively taking control of your personal perceptual filters. You may have inherited the computer operating system from your culture, experience or upbringing but creative visualization provides you with the tools to rewrite your own personal software programmes.

VISUALIZATIONS AND RELATIONSHIPS

You may decide to use creative visualization to improve your relationships with others. You can either do this on your own or with your partner.

* Firstly, decide what goals you have in your relationship. What do you want/need from it? Consider these wants and needs on all levels, be it physical, mental, emotional or spiritual.
* Make your goals specific – this may mean breaking them down into sub-goals. Single sub-goals may be more realistic and easier to achieve.
* Now consider all of the self-limited beliefs and attitudes you have. What kind of things do you say to yourself in your mental dialogue?
* Use affirmations and images to neutralize the negative attitudes and thoughts.
* You may consider exchanging affirmations with your partner. Make an agreement to acknowledge and affirm positive changes.
* Create positive partnership images and affirmations together.

To conclude our brief exploration of creative visualization, I want to consider the spiritual associations of spectrogender.

The spirit of spectrogender

Those of you familiar with literature on Eastern spirituality will have spotted the connections between the three colours assigned to the personality components of spectrogender and the concept of chakras. Chakras are energy centres situated at various points along our bodies. They may be described as spinning wheels of light. There are seven major chakras, each associated with the colour of the light spectrum.

1. **The base or root chakra.** It is associated with the colour red (crimson) and is situated at the base of the spine. Its function is to physically ground us.
2. **The sacral chakra.** It is associated with the colour orange and situated just below the navel. Its function is related to the giving and receiving of sexual pleasure.
3. **The solar plexus chakra.** It is associated with the colour yellow and situated in the mid-line (slightly to the left) of the stomach. It is here that we form opinions (gut reaction).

4. **The heart chakra.** It is associated with the colour green and is the centre for human love (and situated at the heart) Thus it has connections with the green nurture of spectrogender.
5. **The throat chakra.** It is associated with the colour blue. It is related to communication, integrity and vocation (being true to oneself) and is also associated with judgement. It is situated at the throat. Thus, it has a connection with the blue assertiveness of spectrogender.
6. **The brow chakra.** It is sometimes erroneously called the third eye, being in the centre of the forehead and is associated with the colour indigo or deep blue. It is related to clear spiritual insight or vision.
7. **The crown chakra.** It is situated at the top of the head and is often described as the access point to the divine (spiritual) and integrates the physical, mental, emotional and spiritual realms. Its colour is violet.

The two chakras of greatest relevance in terms of spectrogender are the fourth (heart/green) and the fifth (throat/blue). Thus you may want to adapt your creative visualization to account for these two chakras. In terms of sexuality there is a link between the first two chakras (root/red and sacral/orange), so if you are experiencing sexual difficulties, you should focus your creative visualizations on these.

If you are going to work with chakras then buy a dedicated book. To create balance, incorporate a routine to work on all seven chakras in one session, from red through to violet.

Obviously, this brief description has only scratched the surface of chakra knowledge, and indeed about creative visualization. You may consider these techniques and ideas to be too 'far out' for you, but you don't have to buy into the whole philosophy; instead you can use chakras to help you focus your attention and to give more colour to your visualizations.

As the throat chakra symbolizes 'viewpoints', this seems an appropriate place to discuss some techniques for improving communication that are a little more down to earth.

Communication

Communication is (at least) a two-way process. It concerns the exchange of different perspectives, a coming together of personal perceptual filters. It's not just about talking, it's about listening, too. Often it's not what we say but how we say it that determines whether other people will hear us. They may be listening but their personal perceptual filter may cause them to hear what they want to hear. The way you present your message will increase (or decrease) the chances that someone will actually listen and hear you. Moreover, the way you listen will determine whether someone will talk to you.

We often hear a lot about how it's good to talk in relationships. However, when it's time to talk about obstacles or stumbling blocks, it doesn't mean it's time to lump all your petty niggles and resentments into one big amorphous lump and dump it onto a friend, partner or loved one. Even garbage needs to be sorted before it is processed. If your points are really important to you and important to the relationship, then they are worth being treated as matters of importance.

We started by talking about various forms of communication, such as books, plays, films and so on. All these forms went through some editing process to be seen in their best light. There are also communication techniques that help us present our thoughts in the best light. The following suggestions tend to work well when used together and, of course, you need to be flexible and adapt them to your own particular needs, the needs of the other person and the relationship. It's important to remember that there aren't any 'one size fits all' formulae. Be flexible.

Think partnership

* If your relationship is a partnership then you should aim for a win-win situation. It should not be a zero-sum game, where one partner benefits at the expense of the other.
* If you are partners, it's a game of two halves. This means that you really make an effort to see things from each other's perspective.

Pick the right moment

* Don't be tempted to dive in, no matter what the time or place. Agree on a time and place to discuss important matters when you are not likely to be disturbed and without distractions.
* Again, think partnership. It needs to be a time and place that works for both of you that is private and relatively free from stress. You both need to feel safe to disclose your intimate thoughts.
* Don't pick the moment your partner wants to watch his or her favourite programme, when you are on the dance floor at a nightclub or in the frozen food aisle of the supermarket.

Own your statements

* When dealing with negative or difficult issues you need to own your statements. There is a subtle difference between 'I feel' and 'You make me feel'.
* If you introduce a sense of blame, the whole discussion becomes a game of 'emotional poker' in which each partner is trying to outbid the other in the 'hurt' stakes.

The behaviour is not the person

* It is far easier for a person to change their behaviour than to change their whole self. Once you've said: 'You really make me sick', there isn't really anything else left to say, is there?
* If you are on the receiving end, you might want to say: 'In what specific ways do I make you sick?' Prompt for examples as evidence.
* However, if the person says: 'I don't like it when you...' or says how they feel when a particular behaviour occurs, it is more productive as you immediately start talking about the important issues.
* It doesn't have to be all about negative matters, for instead of saying: 'You are useless at foreplay', you could make a point of saying what you do like, for instance: 'I like it when you caress my inner thigh.' Say how good you feel when it happens.
* Psychologically, people respond much better to positive reinforcement, such as praise, than they do to negative feedback, such as 'put downs'.

Observations not judgements

* Don't make sweeping generalized judgements about what things do or don't mean. Don't start sentences with, 'If you loved me', or 'If you cared'. These are not facts, they are about your perceptions.
* Consider this statement: 'You don't care whether or not I get any sexual satisfaction, you just think about yourself.' All wrapped up in one statement is 'caring', 'selfishness' and 'sexual satisfaction'. You may end up arguing about caring and selfishness when you really should be discussing sexual satisfaction.
* Make factual observations not value judgements.

Give specific feedback based on observations

* Words such as 'always', 'sometimes', 'often' and 'never' are rather vague and leave your points wide open for disagreement. Again, it is all about different perspectives.
* You need to put things into context and be more specific. This avoids getting side-tracked by arguing over the terms rather than discussing the real issue.

Share ideas or offer alternatives rather than make demands or give advice

* Most people respond well if they have a sense of input or investment in a course of action. Nobody likes being told what to do, not even schoolchildren. It's about perspectives again.
* Agreeing on the opinions should be a first step in any 'negotiation'. This communicates the idea that you value the other person's point of view. Psychologically, there will be a greater sense of ownership of an idea for both people if they have both contributed to it.

Too much, too soon. Don't go for feedback overload

* When material has a high emotional content, it often takes a little longer to process. So, when a partner discloses something, you may say the first thing that comes into your head or use it as a signal to open up the floodgates, releasing a torrent of emotion.
* As it often requires a little time to 'digest' what you've just heard, sometimes it is important to go away and process the thoughts before 'thinking out loud'. You are less likely to say something that you hadn't thought through fully (and therefore may regret). It is okay to take 'time out' and agree to come back to it.
* If you get into the habit of good communications you will find it is not imperative to have to deal with everything in one go.

Research shows that people who discuss things (even argue) in a similar style are more likely to resolve their differences. Using some or all of these strategies helps to make sure that the right message gets through. It is about learning how to focus on the message rather than getting side-tracked by personal perceptual filters. Essentially, it concerns making your message easier to process by reducing the ambiguity. Of course, this represents an ideal way to communicate and, as we know, sometimes the conditions are not always ideal. So don't worry if you don't put all of these points into action every time.

Research also indicates that people in relationships that are more intimate usually have a number of things in common. They tend to share equally private thoughts and feelings, especially private ones, and are more likely to say 'I love you' or pay their partners a compliment. Couples in intimate relationships are less likely to 'point score' and more likely to seek win-win solutions to any problems. They also tend to take a direct verbal approach rather than expect their partners to be mind-readers and when in conflict they tend to look for a swift resolution rather than 'prolonging the agony'. In short, relationships in which both partners have a balance between assertiveness and nurturance are more intimate and tend to be based on partnership/consensus.

Conclusion: WYSIWYG

Your view of gender roles and relationships has a direct impact on what you get from your relationships and life in general. In this chapter we have examined a number of techniques that you may use to re-tune your personal perceptual filters to androgynous (balanced) gender roles and to relationships based on partnership. What you see is what you get.

In the final chapter we will discuss how the implications of such perspectives affect our attitudes to sex and sexuality.

10

Back To the Future: Changing Views Of Sex, Sexuality and Normality

If sex is such a natural phenomenon, how come there are so many books on how to do it? – Bette Midler, actress (b. 1944)

Nowhere... do the interests of fiction and those of science mingle more intimately than in that body of knowledge we have come to call 'sexuality' – Annie Potts, modern-day gender and sexuality psychologist

Poetry is an orphan of silence. The words never quite equal the experience behind them – Charles Simic, poet (b.1938)

PREVIEW

In this chapter we will:

* Explore the validity of the simple black-and-white labels for sexuality, now that we have begun to challenge binary gender roles.
* Explore the difference between 'doing' and 'being' and between behaviour and attraction.
* Explore the possibility of moving beyond black-and-white categories.

The anatomy of doubt

Hoo-hoos, minkies, willies and winkies,
Who are the 'normals' and who are the 'kinkies'?
Are you heroic Brad or homely Janet,
Or a sweet transvestite from a different planet?
Is it straight-down-the-line or simply confusing?
Is it all in our genes or just something we're choosing?
It is just variation or unholy perversion?
Propagating the species or a fun diversion?
Are you bound by tradition or torn by the doubt,
That we're the ones our parents warned us about?

Sex, drag and gender roles

We often talk about 'doing things by the book'. The crucial question is which book? It makes a big difference. Of course, there has been a proliferation of sex manuals on the market, but these are not the only books that tell us how to 'do it'. There are medical books, psychology books, religious books and law books all telling us the 'right' way to have sex.

Throughout this book we have explored the tenets of the gender-role rulebook and have challenged the view that we can split the world into two clear-cut categories. Our classification of sexuality is also derived from the binary gender system. We often use the euphemism 'swings both ways' instead of bisexual ('bi' describes two options). Although gender and sexuality often seem inextricably linked, recent thinking indicates that they often operate quite independently. Writer and performer Kate Bornstein is a male-to-female-transsexual lesbian illustrating that although her gender changed, her sexuality did not. In interviews she explains that her decision to change gender was affected by the binary gender-role system. At the time she thought that the only alternative to being a man was to become a woman. Her ex-partner writer David Harrison is a female-to-male-trans-sexual gay man, again demonstrating that gender and sexuality are not necessarily linked. Admittedly these are only two examples, however if we look at the world without the binary filter, we find a wealth of material showing that many cultures had third and sometimes fourth gender roles.

Historical travel reports record descriptions of third and fourth gender roles in North and South America, Africa and Asia. For instance, there were

Sex, Lies and Stereotypes

'two-spirits' in many Native American cultures. They were anatomically perfect males (*winkte*) and perfect females (*hwame*) who were distinguished from men and women within the culture in terms of dress, lifestyle and social roles. Two-spirits were often revered but, with the introduction of Christianity and the move away from many-god religions, led to a change in attitudes to gender. Less diversity and attitudes that were more negative to women led to the two-spirits becoming figures of shame. Prior to this cultural shift, for instance, men could form sexual and emotional relationships with two-spirits (*winkte*) without harming their masculine status. Although this may seem alien to modern thinking, it is a relatively recent convention in Western thought that sexuality is determined by our choice of sexual partner.

Changes in the male gender role are almost imperceptible in comparison with changes in the female gender role. The male role is invested with greater power and authority and the change may result in a loss of power. Thus, like some surrogate Atlas, the fantasy is that responsibility for the structure of the world rests on the shoulders of men. We often talk of the double standard whereby sexually 'promiscuous' men are celebrated as 'stallions' and sexually 'promiscuous' women are denounced as 'sluts', 'tarts' and 'slags'. Male bodies are perceived as closed and impenetrable, by contrast women's bodies are seen (usually by men) as open and permeable. Thus 'real' male sexuality is fixed within rigid boundaries, whereas female sexuality is 'open to negotiation'. For men, sexual arousal peaks with penetration. Thus it takes a penis to complete the sex act and anything else is just 'the supporting act' to the 'starring role'. This is why a heterosexual man can 'get off' at the thought of two women having sex. Lesbian sexuality is often viewed (by straight men) as an extension of foreplay. Again, we are faced with a division of labour. Two women can take care of the menial chores and then comes the man to reap the (double) benefits, well at least in the fantasy. The word 'foreplay' suggests a division between the 'warm up' and the 'main event'; many writers have abandoned the use of it in favour of 'sex play'.

There is more at stake because a strong component of attitudes to male homosexuality is the sense of deviation from the narrow confines of the traditional male role. Transcending these restrictions and breaching the boundaries of masculinity represents a challenge to male power. The term 'homosexual' was first used to refer to effeminate men who took the passive role in sex with masculine men. Thus, it was acknowledged that same-sex desire had different meanings for each of the participants. A man who allowed himself to be penetrated by another man undertook the role traditionally ascribed to a female. By contrast, the active partner retained his masculine status, as his role was not substantially changed. It was not until the second decade of the 20th century that both partners engaging in same-sex sexual acts were labelled 'homosexual'. It was then that being a man became synonymous with being 'straight'. Being a man meant 'no sissy stuff' and this meant no same-sex acts.

Although the boundaries were clearly drawn, research into 'homosexual subcultures' in the USA and the UK between the 1920s and the 1940s revealed that some men who were not considered to be 'homosexual' could be 'had' sexually and were referred to as 'trade'. In the late 1940s sex researcher Alfred Kinsey (1894–1956) and colleagues identified men who described themselves as heterosexual but reportedly occasionally 'played the queers'. Today the term 'bi-curious' regularly appears in the 'personal ads' of magazines and newspapers. It denotes heterosexual experimentation rather than a statement of identity. Modern health literature includes the term 'men who have sex with men' (MSM) to refer to heterosexual men who have sex with men, often in public places such as saunas. Much of the early safe-sex literature was aimed at gay and bisexual men. Thus many men who did not identify with either of these labels (but had sex with men) ignored it. There are also those who claim to be gay-for-pay, usually men who claim to be straight but have sex with other men to earn a living. Many authors have questioned the distinction between 'doing' and 'being' gay, that is the difference between behaviour and identity.

Exercise: Blessed/damned

In the exercise below we will extend our exploration of binary categories to sexuality. For each of the pairs, circle one that applies most to you or your life. You may also want to cross out the ones that bear no relation to you or the way you live your life. Now do the exercise.

Good/Bad	Normal/Abnormal	Man/Woman
Blessed/Damned	Straight/Gay	Natural/Unnatural
Married/Unmarried	Paired/Alone	Pairs/Groups
Procreation/Recreation	For love/For money	Hetero/Homo
Non-Commercial/Commercial	Bodies only/With toys	Gendered/Transgendered

In the binary imagination of black-and-white unambiguous classification, you should have circled the first item in each pair. Again, the options reflect a male bias and a heterosexual bias. Many of these binaries derive from the feminist scholar Gayle Rubin's 'hierarchies of shame', in which she contends that we use these as a series of either/or categories to sort the good (blessed) sex from the bad (damned) sex.

The academic Michael Warner in *The Trouble with Normal*, argues that our genitals set up a chain reaction of assumptions, from the way we are supposed to behave through to whom we are supposed to desire and how. Thus, a whole identity is mapped out throughout our lifetime. Whenever we think of heterosexuality we may simply think of a man and a woman having sex. However, Warner argues that heterosexuality is really a label for a whole package of assumptions. It is an attempt to reduce the enormous variety of human capacity and experience into a consensus of a smaller number of possible outcomes. All of these outcomes are supposed to line up and fit together flawlessly. According to this view, heterosexuality is synonymous with good, normal, natural and blessed sexuality.

The term 'vanilla' is often used to describe a 'no frills' approach to sex. Tutti-frutti sex was just included for fun, unless, of course, you know otherwise? We can see that a crossover at any point in these interconnected values (from 'one' to 'zero'), can have a knock-on effect, which Rubin describes as the 'domino theory of sexual peril'. According to Warner, in the world of black-and-white categories with crisp, clear and fixed boundaries, any threat to the integrity of the sequence means that the whole package may be re-combined in boundless ways.

The negative attitudes to bisexuality from straight and gay people alike stems from our belief in the integrity of the blessed/dammed 'hierarchies of shame'. Being gay as the opposite of being straight is a legitimate position in the grand scheme of things. Bisexual people pass back and forth across the boundaries, illustrating that the boundaries aren't really fixed at all.

Monogamous/Promiscuous	Private/Public	Relationship/Casual
Vanilla/Sadomasochist	No-porn/With-porn	Normal/Kinky
Active/Passive	Top/Bottom	Penis/Anus
Lesbian/Gay	Female-anus/Male-anus	Penis/Vagina
Vanilla/Tutti-frutti	Safer/Unsafe	Clean/Dirty
Masculine/Feminine	Sacred/Profane	One/Zero

When I conducted focus groups on attitudes to gender and sexuality with supposedly liberal university students, I was surprised by some of the comments made about bisexual people. Not only were some of the participants oblivious to the fact that someone in the group might be bisexual, they also described bisexuality in the most negative terms. At the very least it was described as experimentation, or a period of transition from straight to gay, or a state of confusion or not wanting to take responsibility. Others speculated that it was just 'the tip of the iceberg' and indicative of underlying personality problems.

Bi-curious implicitly recognizes the binary law or either/or and 'owns up' to 'curiosity' and 'experimentation'. The attitudes from my focus groups are fairly typical of the way in which bisexuality is viewed. It is often characterized by references to confusion, immaturity, insecurity, sexual obsession and immorality, shallowness and fickleness. In lesbian and gay communities, bisexuality is often viewed with suspicion or even associated with betrayal. Terms such as 'batting for both teams', 'best of both worlds' and 'sits on both sides of the church' all indicate conflict of interests, divided loyalties or outright treachery. References in gay personal ads to 'straight-acting' or 'non-camp' suggest another way in which some gay men subscribe to the 'hierarchies of shame'.

In chapter 2 we discussed at length our personal and cultural intolerance of ambiguity. Negative attitudes to bisexuality represent our fear of 'the space between' categories, another way in which we enforce the law of excluded middle.

The word 'gospel' from 'godspell' means 'good news' and the German root of the English word 'good' comes from *gath* which means 'to bring together'. Our word 'gathering' has the same origin. Goodliness, godliness and gathering together are linked, just like the ones and zeroes in our binary categories. The English word for 'bad' has its origins in the Old English word *baeddel* or *baedling* meaning a womanish man. Thus, an unmanly man is the personification of badness. This helps us see that negative attitudes to homosexuality (homophobia) are, in part, based, on our attitudes to deviation from the traditional male gender role.

Homophobia is really an extension of negative attitudes to femininity (sexism). Gender and sexuality are based on male values. Heterosexuality and masculinity are inextricably linked. Gay men transgress the gender boundaries in the act of anal intercourse, the one being penetrated (passive/bottom/Martha) is thought of as performing the female role. He chooses to relinquish his birthright. We use genital shape as a metaphor for

Sex, Lies and Stereotypes

organizing gender roles. The traditional male role is all about the impenetrability of the masculine psychological armour (and body). It's about being a tough guy, a big shot and a hell raiser but no 'girly stuff'. 'Real' masculinity is supposed to be perfect but homosexuality, the Achilles heel of masculinity, serves to remind us that it is flawed. The anus represents the point where masculinity can be breached: the 'Achilles Hole'. Homosexuality seems to advertise this fact. Again, similarity overrides difference.

I anticipate that for some tastes there will be too much talk of 'gayness and anus'. However, the issue is not really that there is too much discussion of these topics but rather that they have been discussed at all.

Beyond binary

In the mid-20th century, when George Orwell was writing about Big Brother, Sex Crimes, Room 101 and imaginary wars that unified opinions, an academic book became a bestseller. Usually such books sell a moderate number of copies within the academic world, but this particular book caught the imagination of the public at large. The book was *Sexual Behavior in the Human Male* by Alfred Kinsey and his colleagues.

The book challenged many common-sense notions of sexuality, most notably that we could only divide men into two categories: those who had sex with women (heterosexual) and those who had sex with men (homosexual). Instead, it proposed a whole spectrum of sexuality. Five years later, in the early 1950s, the Kinsey team offered the companion volume *Sexual Behavior in the Human Female* and used the same classification for female sexuality.

Kinsey's work was published around the same time that other researchers (mentioned in chapter 2) were looking at the nature of attitudes, prejudice and personality and how the Western mind prefers black-and-white categories. Instead of binary categories, Kinsey and colleagues offered a continuum of seven different types of sexuality, ranging from 'exclusively heterosexual' to 'exclusively homosexual', with five degrees of bisexuality in between. Equal attraction to men and women is rated 3, whereas 2 and 4 represent a slight preference for women or men. Thus someone who describes themselves as bi-curious would equate a 1, where the homosexual attraction or behaviour would be described as 'incidental'.

0____1____2____3____4____5____6
Heterosexual　　　　Bisexual　　　　Homosexual

 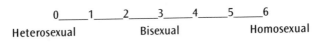

More than half a century after the publication of these two volumes, we still cling to the old categories of 'straight' or 'gay'. Although the Kinsey rating scheme offered some development in our appreciation of human sexuality, it did not separate attraction from behaviour. Research suggests that, although connected, attraction and behaviour do not match perfectly. Surveys have shown a notable discrepancy, suggesting that many more people are attracted to their own sex but don't necessarily act upon it. One study of over 6,000 men and women in the USA, UK and France found just that. When men were asked if they had engaged in any same-sex acts (since the age of 15), almost 6 per cent said yes. However, when asked whether they had engaged in same-sex acts or had been attracted to their own sex, the figure rose more than three-fold to 18.5 per cent. This figure suggests that there are a lot of bi-curious people out there. More importantly, it demonstrates that sexual attraction and sexual behaviour, at least for some people, are separate concepts. Thus some researchers use the Kinsey scale to take separate measures of attraction and behaviour to account for this difference.

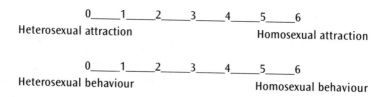

0_____1_____2_____3_____4_____5_____6
Heterosexual attraction   Homosexual attraction

0_____1_____2_____3_____4_____5_____6
Heterosexual behaviour   Homosexual behaviour

Other researchers have offered further refinements with seven different subscales, each rated on the Kinsey seven-point scale. Theses are:

1. Sexual attraction.
2. Sexual behaviour.
3. Sexual fantasy.
4. Emotional preference.
5. Social preference.
6. Self-identification.
7. Hetero/gay lifestyle.

Imagine the personal ads:

Fun loving 6653363 seeks similar for fun and friendship. No 6663366's need apply.

Couple of 3333333's looking for a 4444444 or a 2222222 to spice up our three-ish lives.

The scheme has its good points because it separates attraction, behaviour and other labels we use to describe ourselves. However, it also introduces problems by assuming that there is such a thing as a heterosexual or gay lifestyle, and that these abstract phrases mean the same thing to all people. It also presents the concepts of 'social preference' for spending time with men or women. Although it attempts to move beyond binary thinking, it actually succeeds in emphasizing it.

More PoMo than homo

PoMo is short for 'postmodern', the word that designers like to slip into the conversation to make disaster appear like intent. It concerns rejecting the inevitable sequence of expectations; it borrows from styles and fuses them together. Thus, postmodern architecture combines ancient with modern, abstract with concrete (lots of concrete) and the familiar with the unfamiliar that manages to surprise, confuse, horrify and reassure us, all at the same time. Once upon a time everything had a name, a place and a function. Everything ran like clockwork and was done by the book. Everything was in black and white, all the binary zeroes lined up, all the binary ones lined up and we all lived happily ever after.

Consider the zeroes/ones exercise in chapter 2 and the blessed/ damned exercise in this chapter. The values are all supposed to line up in a predicable sequence, but what if the either/or categories are replaced with seven-point rating scales? Now imagine we allow free movement between the 'good' and the 'bad' side and the opportunity to 'inhabit' the middle ground. While this would more accurately reflect the infinite variation in sexuality and gender identity, it would make it difficult to draw a line between 'good' and 'bad'. This renders the system of classification meaningless, so why not abandon it altogether?

Pomosexuality (postmodern sexuality) is not so much about 'throwing the baby out with the bath water', it's about throwing out the bath as well. We often use the phrase 'singing from the same hymn sheet' to indicate that we all share the same vision or model of the world. Pomosexuality serves to remind us that our words or models never quite equal the experience behind them. Our binary models of gender and sexuality both reflect and reinforce power structures in our dominator-focused, hierarchical societies. However, what we all have in common is that none of us perfectly matched the binary ideals. We vary in how different we are from the extreme poles of binary categories. However, we are only united in the fact that we do differ.

Challenging the fixed notions of gender and sexuality and the connections between them opens up the 'zone of possibility', the middle ground in which we live out our everyday lives. We know that masculinity and femininity are affected by different situations. We know our sexual preferences, tastes and orientations vary from person to person. So, can people have sex without it constituting part of their identity?

We have begun to embrace a more diverse vision of gender and sexuality evidenced by the numerous terms by which we identify ourselves. New men, new women, lads, new lads, ladettes, gay straight, bisexual, bi-curious, transsexual, transgendered, MSM and the curious classifications in the personal ads. Sex means different things to different people. Even if we do it by the book, people may have very different motivations for doing the same thing. Furthermore, the same sex act may evoke different emotions. For some people it has nothing to do with identity while for others it is everything.

In chapter 4, we reviewed the biological evidence that transfers the emphasis from a male-centred view of gender and sexuality onto a female-centred view – the clitoris is solely for sexual pleasure. So, how can we even begin to answer the question 'what causes sexuality?' until we solve the enigma of the clitoris and the human capacity for anal erotic pleasure? If sex is just about having babies, why don't we just get it over quickly as and when necessary? People never 'just' have sex. It always brims with significance. It is never just about one thing. Sometimes it simply defies explanation.

Conclusion: Back to the future

In this chapter, we have explored the connection between sex, gender and sexuality. Ultimately, if we challenge the fundamental units of gender (man and woman), this must have a knock-on effect for sex and sexuality. If we accept that two men can be very different, if those two men have sex does this make them 'homosexual' because 'homo' means 'same'? If a man and a woman have sex are they automatically 'heterosexual', because 'hetero' means different? Do such labels serve any purpose or would be better off without them? Does the label add anything to your life? Surely the criteria should be that if *consenting adults* want to have sex, they should just take care of their sexual health. So, isn't it time we let blessed sexuality go 'swing'?

Conclusion

Men are from Earth, Women are from Earth. Get Over It!

Two things inspire me to awe – the starry heavens and the moral universe within – Albert Einstein, physicist (1879–1955)

It is not in the stars to hold our destiny but in ourselves – William Shakespeare, English playwright (1564–1616)

A declaration of interdependence

We, the people of planet Earth, have an inherent need to make sense of the Universe and to discover our place in the grand scheme of things. In many ways, each of us is our own centre of the Universe. We are the leading lights and the starring roles in our own life stories. However, sometimes we need to become the satellites and orbit other stars and planets. Essential to the human project is the ability to negotiate the attraction of other celestial bodies, other stars just like us.

So, we are about to complete our orbit of the world of gender and relationships. Fond of doing things by the book, we have visited the Good Book, the science books, the psychology books, the biology books and some less erudite ones too. We've had close encounters with the 'ins and outs' of sex, with the lies and half-truths that distort our view of the world and with the stereotypes to which we are expected to conform. And now, we've come full circle, back to women, men and planets, or rather this planet.

Men are from Earth, women are from Earth. Isn't it time we just got over it and moved on? Of course, it's easy to understand the appeal of some pop-psychology books that present us with the 'science fiction' rather than the scientific facts. They seem to satisfy our need for simplicity, structure and romance. However, the scientific facts are sometimes far more romantic than anything dreamed of in the pop-psychology imagination.

When the Universe began with the Big Bang, it took a while for things to get started, as there was little in the way of chemistry between the main elements. Only with the birth and death of the large stars did the story really begin. A supernova occurs at the end of a star's lifetime, when its fuel is exhausted and can no longer support its release of energy. The blast from the explosion and its collapse ploughs the star's atmosphere into space, driving elements such as gold and uranium outward, where they mingle with other matter to form brand new stars. Our Sun is made up of third-generation material, having been part of two previous stars. By chance or by design, the chemistry was right to form solid planets like the Earth, which is rich in precious elements, such as gold. So, the calcium in our bones, the iron in our blood and the rings on our fingers were all forged in the stars. We are, indeed, stardust.

The lyrics of a Joni Mitchell (b.1943) song are both poetic and scientific: 'We are stardust, we are golden/And we got to get ourselves back to the garden'. Going back to the garden does not mean going back to the comfort zone of our backyards; we need to go back to basics, back to new ground rules for new men and new women in a new Eden. We've seen that partnership precedes domination from biological, historical, theological, psychological and cosmological perspectives. However, we do not view the world through pristine eyes. We impose structure and introduce distortions, through various filters, on the kaleidoscopic flux of impressions that impinge upon us. But if we have to look back to the halcyon days, then why can't we do so through a filter of stardust rather than star wars?

Our current gender system emphasizes our differences and suppresses our similarities. We are undoubtedly more similar than different, but we reorganize nature and our perceptions into a hierarchical black-and-white, all-or-nothing, zero-sum game. Divided and alienated, rather than united, we are left with dominance and submission, rather than mutual inter-dependence. We remain two halves that never feel quite whole.

Sex, Lies and Stereotypes

Surely each of us needs to value and embrace the whole of the human experience irrespective of the arbitrary names and divisions that we impose upon it. Will our human qualities, experiences, dreams and ambitions always be encapsulated in our genital shape? Are gender, sexuality and relationships destined forever to be a matter of 'role, pole and hole'? Are we resigned to this illusory anatomical destiny? Do we have a part in its perpetuation or in its re-creation? Are we destined to be trapped in a gender (political) timewarp? It's just a step to the left and then a step to the right; one small step forward and a giant leap back. Aren't the science fantasy metaphors wearing thin?

And so we return to the question: Are you one of the girls, one of the boys, one in a million or just one of the guys? Are you traditionally gendered, your own immaculate conception, or rarely give it a second thought? I'd like to conclude with an excerpt from a memo that was sent from an employer in response to an employee about sexual harassment and subsequently circulated on the internet. It highlights that it is not always easy to think outside rigid boundaries, nevertheless, what matters is that we keep trying.

> I fully realize that I have not succeeded in answering your questions. Indeed, I feel I have not answered any of them completely. The answers I have found only serve to raise a whole new set of questions, which only lead to more problems, some of which we weren't even aware were problems. To sum it all up... In some ways I feel we are more confused than ever, but I believe we are now confused on a higher level, and about more important issues.

Be assured that the smallest of personal changes to your 'director's cut' in your gender-role movie may have profound effects, even if it's just a change of lighting. In times of change it's the learners who inherit the Earth. And with the thought that a 'head in the clouds' is better than a 'head in the sand', I'll leave you with the words of the poet Robert Browning (1812–89), embraced by Anigavlian and Sineplian alike:

Our reach should exceed our grasp. Or what's a heaven for?

Notes and Further Reading

CHAPTER ONE

For terminology see: Bornstein, K. (1998), *My Gender Workbook*, London: Routledge; Burr, V. (1998), *Gender and Social Psychology*, London: Routledge; Strong, B. & DeVault, C. (1997), *Human Sexuality. Diversity in Contemporary America*, London: Mayfield Publishing Company; and Stainton Rogers, W. & Stainton Rogers, R. (2001), *The Psychology of Gender and Sexuality*, Buckingham: Open University Press. For slang for genitalia see: Braun, V. and Kitzinger, C. (2001), '"Snatch", or "Hole", or "Honey-pot"? Semantic Categories and the Problem of Nonspecificity in Female Genital Slang', *Journal of Sex Research*, May 2001 – see www.findarticles.com

CHAPTER TWO

Sources for 'Ways of Viewing the World' quiz include: Budner, S. (1962), 'Intolerance of Ambiguity as a Personality Variable', *Journal of Personality*, Vol.33, pp.476–511; Nueberg, S.L. & Newson, J.T. (1993), 'Personal Need for Structure: Individual Differences in the Desire for Simple Structure', *Journal of Personality and Social Psychology*, Vol.65, pp.113–31, and Wrightsman, L.S. (1992), *Assumptions about Human Nature. Implications for Researchers and Practitioners* (2nd edn), London: Sage. For one-god/many-god religions see: Hoffman, R.J. (1984), 'Vices, Gods and Virtues: Cosmology as a Mediating Factor in Attitudes toward Homosexuality', *Journal of Homosexuality*, Vol.9, pp.27–44.

CHAPTER THREE

For gender filters (lenses) see: Bem, S.L. (1993), *The Lenses of Gender: Transforming the Debate on Sexual Inequality*, New Haven: Yale University Press.

For 'real men' and 'real women' see: Brannon, R.(1976), 'The Male Sex Role: Our Culture's Blueprint for Manhood and What It's Done For Us Lately', in D.S. David and R. Brannon (eds), *The Forty-nine percent Majority*, Reading, MA: Addison-Wesley; and Welter, B. (1978), 'The Cult of True Womanhood: 1830–1860', in M.Gordon (ed.), *The American Family in Socio-historical Perspective* (2nd edn), New York: St Martin's Press.

For 'androgyny' see: Bem, S.L. (1974), 'The measurement of psychological androgyny', *Journal of Consulting and Clinical Psychology*, Vol.42, pp.325–54.

CHAPTER FOUR

For chromosomes see: Plant, S. (1998), *Zeroes + Ones. Digital Women and the New Technoculture*, London: Fourth Estate; and Stainton Rogers, W. & Stainton Rogers, R. (2001), *The Psychology of Gender and Sexuality*, Buckingham: Open University Press.

For anal anatomy see: Agnew, J. (1986), 'Anatomical and Physiological Aspects of Anal Sex Practices', *Journal of Homosexuality*, VOL.12, pp.75–96; Marcio, J., Jorge, N. & Wexner, S.D. (1997), 'Anatomy and Physiology of Rectum and Anus', *European Journal of Surgery*, Vol.163, pp.723–31; Morin, J. (1998), *Anal Pleasure and Health. A Guide for Men and Women*, San Francisco: Down There Press; and Ooi, B.S., Ho, Y.H., Eu, K.W., Nyam, D., Leong, A & Seow-Choen, F. (1998), 'Management of Anorectal Foreign Bodies: A Cause of Obscure Anal Pain', *Australian and New Zealand Journal of Surgery*, Vol.68, pp.852–853.

Emily Martin's work is summarized in Eisler, R. (1995), *Sacred Pleasure. Sex, Myth, and the Politics of the Body*, Dorset: Element Books.

CHAPTER FIVE

For gender differences see: Basow, S.A. (1992), *Gender Stereotypes and Roles* (3rd edn), California: Brooks/Cole Publishing; Burr, V. (1998), *Gender and Social Psychology*, London: Routledge; Stainton Rogers, W. & Stainton Rogers, R. (2001), *The Psychology of Gender and Sexuality*, Buckingham: Open University Press and Strong, B. & DeVault, C. (1997), *Human Sexuality. Diversity in Contemporary America*, London: Mayfield Publishing Company for guidelines to assess research.

CHAPTER SIX

For health implications of gender roles see Basow, S.A. (1992), *Gender Stereotypes and Roles* (3rd edn), California: Brooks/Cole Publishing; Doyal, L. (1995), *What Makes Women Sick. Gender and the Political Economy of Health*, London: Macmillan Press; Lee, C. and Owens, R.G. (2002), *The Psychology of Men's Health*, Buckingham: Open University Press.

CHAPTER SEVEN

For partnership-based relationships see: Riane Eisler (1987, 1998), *The Chalice and the Blade*, London:Thorsons/ Harper Collins, and Riane Eisler. (2002), T*he Power of Partnership. Seven Relationships That Will Change Your Life*, California: New World.

CHAPTER EIGHT

For 'chromatic' gender see Rothblatt, M. (1996), *The Apartheid of Sex. A Manifesto on the Freedom of Gender*, London: Pandora.

CHAPTER NINE

For creative visualization see: Gawain, S. (1982), *Creative Visualization*, London: Bantam Books.

For chakras see: Davies, B. (1998), *The Rainbow Journey. Seven Steps to Self Healing*, London: London Coronet/ Hodder and Stoughton.

CHAPTER TEN

For blessed/damned sexuality see: Rubin, G. (1984, 1993), 'Thinking Sex. Notes for a Radical Theory of the Politics of Sexuality', in Abelove, H., Barale, M.A., & Halperin, D.M. (eds), *The Lesbian & Gay Studies Reader*, London: Routledge; Warner, M. (1994), *The Trouble With Normal. Sex, Politics and the Ethics of Queer Life*, New York: The Free Press.

For differences between sexual behaviour and attraction see: Sell, R.L., Wells, J.A. & Wypij, D. (1995), 'The Prevalence of Homosexual Behaviour and Attraction in the United States, the United Kingdom, and France: Results of National Population-Based Samples', *Archives of Sexual Behaviour*, Vol.24, pp.235–48.

For sexual identity see: Shively, M.G. & DeCecco, J.P. (1977), 'Components of Sexual Identity', *Journal of Homosexuality*, Vol.3, pp.41–8; Klein, F., Sepekoff, B. & Wolf, T.J. (1985), 'Sexual Orientation: A Multi-Variable Dynamic Process', *Journal of Homosexuality*, Vol.11, pp.35–49.

WEBSITES

Kathleen Trigiani's *Out of the Cave: Exploring Gray's Anatomy* at
http://web2.iadfw.net/ktrig246/out_of_cave/

Susan Hamson's *Rebuttal from Uranus* at
http://ourworld.compuserve.com/homepages/women_rebuttal_from_uranus/

  Sex, Lies and Stereotypes